SCHOLASTIC

Research-Based Reading Lessons for K-3

MAUREEN McLAUGHLIN
LESLIE FISHER

New York • Toronto • London • Auckland • Sydney
Mexico City • New Delhi • Hong Kong • Buenos Aires

Teaching *Resources*

Acknowledgments

As always, there are many people to thank for making this book possible. We acknowledge them now for their contributions, but most especially for their enthusiasm and keen ability to find humor despite looming deadlines.

We are particularly grateful to the following people:

Our families and friends for their extraordinary patience and support

Our contributing teachers, reading specialists, coaches, and administrators:
AMY HOMEYER, Roxbury School District, New Jersey
JENNIFER SASSAMAN, Roxbury School District, New Jersey
ED ABATO, Mendham Borough School District, New Jersey
ALICE CYPHERS, Bangor Area School District, Pennsylvania
ALISON SUGRA, Northampton Area School District, Pennsylvania
EVERENE DOWNING, Trenton Public Schools, New Jersey
VENETTA HURLEY, Trenton Public Schools, New Jersey
ANNE HORNE, Trenton Public Schools, New Jersey
MARGE DEVENNIE, Trenton Public Schools, New Jersey
DONNA DONOHUE-COLUMBUS, Trenton Public Schools, New Jersey
JENNIFER LaGRASSA, Trenton Public Schools, New Jersey
KAREN WIDMER, Stroudsburg Area School District, Pennsylvania
JENNIFER FORNATARO, Stroudsburg Area School District, Pennsylvania
FLORA DOWNING HALL, Stroudsburg Area School District, Pennsylvania
GARY SCHUBERT, Stroudsburg Area School District, Pennsylvania
TERRY COOPER, Vice President and Editor in Chief, Scholastic Inc.
JOANNA DAVIS-SWING, Executive Editor, Scholastic Inc.
EILEEN HILLEBRAND, Vice President, Sales and Marketing, Scholastic Inc.
SUSAN KOLWICZ, Senior Marketing Manager, Scholastic Inc.
MARIA LILJA, Senior Designer, Scholastic Inc.
MARGERY ROSNICK, Acquisitions Editor, Scholastic Inc.
KIM BAYER, STACEY SHAREK, and LYNN WARD, special assistants

"Mice" by Rose Fyleman. Copyright © 1932 by Doubleday. Reprinted by permission of Doubleday.

"That Cat!" by Jaime Lucero. Copyright © 2002 by Jaime Lucero. Reprinted by permission of Scholastic Inc.

Readers Theater script on page 98 adapted from *Wolf!* by Becky Bloom, illustrated by Pascal Biet. Copyright (c) 1999 by Siphano, Montpellier. Reprinted by permission of Orchard Books, published by Scholastic Inc.

Readers Theater script on page 102 adapted from *What's the Time Grandma Wolf?* by Ken Brown, published by Peachtree publishers, first published by Andersen Press Ltd., London. Used with permission.

Cover and interior design by Maria Lilja
Cover photograph © PictureQuest-22309072/McLean, VA

ISBN: 0-439-75462-3

2 3 4 5 6 7 8 9 10   40   11 10 09 08 07 06 05

Contents

Introduction 5

CHAPTER ONE: Teaching Research-Based Reading
in the Primary Grades 6

The Guided Comprehension Model for the Primary Grades 7
Final Thoughts on This Chapter 12

CHAPTER TWO: Phonemic Awareness 14

Part One: Research Base 15
Part Two: Lesson Overview 17
Lesson 1: Phoneme Isolation 18
Lesson 2: Phoneme Identity 23
Lesson 3: Phoneme Categorization 28
Lesson 4: Phoneme Blending 35
Lesson 5: Phoneme Segmentation 40
Lesson 6: Phoneme Deletion and Addition 44
Final Thoughts on This Chapter 48

CHAPTER THREE: Phonics 50

Part One: Research Base 51
Part Two: Lesson Overview 52
Lesson 1: Alphabet Letters and Sounds 53
Lesson 2: Making Words 60
Lesson 3: Making and Writing Words 63
Lesson 4: Guess the Covered Word 66
Lesson 5: Onset/Rime Word Wall 70
Lesson 6: Word Families 74
Final Thoughts on This Chapter 78

CHAPTER FOUR: Fluency 80

Part One: Research Base 81
Part Two: Lesson Overview 82
Lesson 1: The Fluent Reading Model 83
Lesson 2: Echo Reading 88
Lesson 3: Choral Reading 91
Lesson 4: Repeated Reading 94
Lesson 5: Readers Theater 97
Final Thoughts on This Chapter 105

CHAPTER FIVE: Vocabulary 106

    Part One: Research Base 107
    Part Two: Lesson Overview 108
    Lesson 1: Semantic Maps 109
    Lesson 2: Concept of Definition Maps 115
    Lesson 3: Synonym Rhymes 121
    Lesson 4: Semantic Question Maps 125
    Lesson 5: Vocabulary Bookmark Technique 130
    Final Thoughts on This Chapter 135

CHAPTER SIX: Comprehension 136

    Part One: Research Base 137
    Part Two: Lesson Overview 138
    Lesson 1: Story Impressions 140
    Lesson 2: "I Wonder" Statements 146
    Lesson 3: Drawing Connections 151
    Lesson 4: Draw and Label Visualizations 155
    Lesson 5: Bookmark Technique 161
    Lesson 6: Draw and Label Retelling 165
    Lesson 7: Discussion Web 170
    Final Thoughts on This Chapter 175

CONCLUSION: Continuing the Journey 176

Appendices 177

    A. Books That Promote Phonemic Awareness, Phonics,
       and Fluency 177
    B. Ideas for Teaching Phonemic Awareness 179
    C. Ideas for Teaching Phonics 182
    D. Ideas for Creating Word Walls 184
    E. Ideas for Teaching Fluency 188
    F. Comprehension Strategies, Teaching Ideas, and Blacklines 189
    G. Center Planner and Student Self-Assessment 217

References 219

Index 223

Introduction

If you are a primary grade teacher, reading specialist, reading coach, curriculum specialist, school administrator, pre-service teacher, or teacher educator, this book is for you. It will take you beyond the activity books and provide you with a clear understanding of phonemic awareness, phonics, fluency, vocabulary, and comprehension.

We wrote this book as a practical guide for teaching reading in the primary grades. We begin with a research-based discussion of current trends in teaching reading. In Chapters 2 through 6, we examine each of the five building blocks of literacy—phonemic awareness, phonics, fluency, vocabulary, and comprehension. We explain each component, delineate its research base, present a sound instructional format, offer practical ideas for teaching, provide numerous classroom-tested lessons, and give suggestions for further reading. In the Conclusion we share our thoughts on teaching reading in current times. The appendices provide resources such as book lists, detailed descriptions of comprehension strategies, related blackline masters, and guidelines for planning literacy centers and word walls.

We hope you will find this book to be an indispensable resource—one that will inform your teaching and contribute to your ever-increasing understanding of the reading process. We thank you for joining us in our continuing quest to become excellent reading teachers—educators who won't settle for anything less than all of our students achieving their greatest possible potential.

Maureen and Leslie

CHAPTER 1

Teaching Research-Based Reading in the Primary Grades

As teachers of reading, we know all too well the need to keep pace with developments in literacy. We want to know which components of the reading process should be emphasized in instruction and how best to teach them. We know that phonemic awareness, phonics, fluency, vocabulary, and comprehension are the current research emphases in the primary grades.

Each of these literacy components contributes to readers' understanding of text. Phonemic awareness enables the reader to differentiate between and among sounds. Phonics is a way of teaching reading that combines phonemes (sounds) and graphemes (written letters) to help readers pronounce words. Fluency, or reading with expression, helps the reader to move beyond word-by-word reading in order to comprehend the text. Vocabulary, understanding the meaning of words, is an essential component of comprehension—the process through which the reader constructs meaning. Research supports that phonemic awareness, phonics, fluency, vocabulary, and comprehension can and should be taught.

In this volume, we focus on three aspects of teaching these building blocks of literacy: (1) reporting what the research has to say, (2) providing a well-established instructional framework for teaching, and (3) presenting classroom-taught lessons that feature teacher think-alouds and examples of student work.

The research base and lessons differ for each component and, consequently, are presented separately in Chapters 2, 3, 4, 5, and 6, each of which addresses a specific element. The teaching framework and its theoretical underpinnings, which provide the instructional foundation of all of the lessons, are detailed in the following section.

The Guided Comprehension Model for the Primary Grades

The instructional framework used to create the lessons in this volume is the Guided Comprehension Model for the Primary Grades (McLaughlin, 2003). It is a three-stage process focused on direct and guided instruction, application, and reflection (see Figure 1-1). The model progresses in the following sequence:

STAGE ONE:	Teacher-directed whole-group instruction
STAGE TWO:	Comprehension strategy practice in teacher-guided small groups and student-facilitated comprehension centers and routines
STAGE THREE:	Teacher-facilitated whole-group reflection and goal setting

FIGURE 1-1

Overview of Guided Comprehension Instruction

(adapted from McLaughlin, 2003)

STAGE 1

Teacher-Directed Whole-Group Instruction:

Teaching a comprehension strategy using easy, instructional, or challenging text.

EXPLAIN the strategy and how it relates to the class goal.

DEMONSTRATE the strategy using a think-aloud and a read-aloud.

GUIDE student practice by reading additional sections of text aloud and having students apply the strategy with support. Monitor students' application.

PRACTICE by having students apply the strategy to another section of text you have read, providing minimal support. Application can occur in small groups or pairs.

REFLECT by having students think about what they know and how they can use this strategy on their own.

STAGE 2

Students apply the comprehension strategies in teacher-guided small groups and student-facilitated comprehension centers and routines. In these settings, students work with varying levels of support and use appropriate instructional- and independent-level texts.

Teacher-Guided Small-Group Instruction:

Applying comprehension strategies with teacher guidance using instructional-level texts and dynamic grouping (four to six students).

REVIEW previously taught strategies and focus on the current strategy and teaching idea.

GUIDE students to apply the strategy as well as previously taught strategies as they read a section of the instructional level text. Prompt students to construct and share personal meanings. Scaffold as necessary, gradually releasing support as students become more proficient. Encourage discussion and repeat with other sections of text.

PRACTICE by having students work in pairs or individually to apply the strategy. Encourage discussion. Have students record their strategy applications in their Guided Comprehension Journals and share them with the class during Stage 3.

REREAD, RETELL & REFLECT by having students engage in a second reading of the text, retell what they have read, and share ways in which the strategy helped them to understand the text. Talk about ways in which students can apply the strategy in comprehension centers and routines.

Student-Facilitated Comprehension Centers and Routines:
Applying comprehension strategies individually, in pairs, or in small groups using independent-level texts.

COMPREHENSION CENTERS are purposeful, authentic, independent settings that provide opportunities to practice strategy application and extend understanding.

COMPREHENSION ROUTINES are procedures that foster habits of thinking and processing that aid in comprehension of text, such as Cross-Age Reading Experiences and Literature Circles.

(STAGE 3)

Teacher-Facilitated Whole-Group Reflection and Goal Setting:
Reflecting on performance, sharing experiences, and setting new goals.

SHARE performances from Stage 2.
REFLECT on ability to use the strategy.
SET NEW GOALS or extend existing ones.

Assessment Options: *Use authentic measures in all stages.*

The structure of the model supports scaffolded teaching and learning. It begins with explicit whole-group instruction during Stage 1. In this stage, the teacher provides a great deal of support, including read-alouds and think-alouds, during the "Explain" and "Demonstrate" steps. This support may gradually lessen as the students work in small groups or pairs in the "Guide" step and may decrease even more in the "Practice" step, when students might progress from working in small groups to working in pairs, or from working in pairs to working individually. In the "Reflect" step, the teacher and students openly discuss what has been learned.

In Stage 2, students experience three settings: small-group guided instruction with the teacher; independent practice with a partner or individually in the comprehension centers; and independent practice in pairs or small groups in comprehension routines, such as Cross-Age Reading Experiences and Literature Circles. All students engage in small-group guided instruction with the teacher, but while one group is with the teacher, the other students work in centers or routines.

Having three different settings operating during Stage 2 may seem challenging from an organizational standpoint, but it is reasonably easy to manage when an organizational plan is in place. Figure 1-2 shows what we believe is the best way to organize for Stage 2. This chart, which can be hung on the classroom wall, shows where everyone in the class should be during Stage 2. It is important to teach students how to read the chart and use it every day to know their scheduled locations. For example, Mary Ellen might look for her name on the chart and learn that she should report to guided reading group first, and when that is over, she should go to the theme center. Similarly, Steven might look for his name and learn that he should report to cross-age reading experience first and then go to guided reading. Students quickly learn to look for their names and understand where they should be when. Students move when a guided reading group concludes. Since guided small groups generally last for about 20 minutes, students change locations approximately every 20 minutes.

FIGURE 1-2

Organizing and Managing Stage 2

	Session 1	Session 2
CENTERS		
ABC Center		
Drama Center		
Listening Center		
Making and Writing Words Center		
Writing Center		
ROUTINES		
Cross-Age Reading Experiences		
Literature Circles		
TEACHER-GUIDED SMALL GROUPS		

In Stage 3, another whole-group setting, students share the work they completed in Stage 2. Then the teacher and students reflect on what they have learned and decide whether to extend the current goal or create a new one.

In addition to providing a framework for teaching, the Guided Comprehension Model for the Primary Grades offers numerous opportunities for informal assessment. For example, in Stage 1, we can use observation of student responses (oral, written, dramatized, sketched) and work habits to assess. In Stage 2's teacher-guided small groups, we can ask the students to whisper read, so we can assess their fluency. We can also do running records in this setting. When the students are working independently in the centers and routines, we can assess their completed work and review their self-assessments (see My Center and Routine Assessment in Appendix G, p. 218). The results of these assessments give direction to our teaching. For example, the results of a running record may indicate a need to move a student to a higher guided reading group.

The Guided Comprehension Model for the Primary Grades is underpinned by current beliefs about literacy. These include that good readers are active and strategic (Askew & Fountas, 1998), motivation and engagement are essential to the reading process (Gambrell, 1996; Guthrie & Wigfield, 2000), reading comprehension skills and strategies can be taught—beginning in the primary grades (Hilden & Pressley, 2002; McLaughlin, 2003), multiple types and levels of texts should be taught (Fountas & Pinnell, 1999), and assessment is a dynamic process (McLaughlin, 2003).

Final Thoughts on This Chapter

This chapter has provided an overview of our text and has shared essential beliefs about the research-based Guided Comprehension Model for the Primary Grades, which serves as the instructional framework for the lessons featured in Chapters 2 through 6. Figure 1-3 shows an overview of the lessons, topics, and teaching ideas in those chapters.

In the next chapter, we begin our exploration of the building blocks of literacy by examining phonemic awareness. We present research-based information about phonemic awareness and provide six lessons that demonstrate how to teach it.

FIGURE 1-3

Overview of Lessons in Chapters 2–6

	CHAPTERS				
	2 Phonemic Awareness	**3** Phonics	**4** Fluency	**5** Vocabulary	**6** Comprehension
1	Phonemic Isolation (p. 18)	Alphabet Letters and Sounds (p. 53)	Fluent Reading Models (p. 83)	Semantic Maps (p. 109)	Story Impressions (p. 140)
2	Phoneme Identity (p. 23)	Making Words (p. 60)	Echo Reading (p. 88)	Concept of Definition Maps (p. 115)	"I Wonder" Statements (p. 146)
3	Phoneme Categorization (p. 28)	Making and Writing Words (p. 63)	Choral Reading (p. 91)	Synonym Rhymes (p. 121)	Drawing Connections (p. 151)
4	Phoneme Blending (p. 35)	Guess the Covered Word (p. 66)	Repeated Readings (p. 94)	Semantic Question Maps (p. 125)	Draw and Label Visualizations (p. 155)
5	Phoneme Segmentation (p. 40)	Onset/Rime Word Wall (p. 70)	Readers Theater (p. 97)	Vocabulary Bookmark Technique (p. 130)	Bookmark Technique (p. 161)
6	Phoneme Deletion and Addition (p. 44)	Word Families (p. 74)			Draw and Label Retelling (p. 165)
7					Discussion Web (p. 170)

(Left side vertical label: **LESSONS**)

CHAPTER 2

Phonemic Awareness

Phonemic awareness has long been understood as a component of reading, but it has received renewed attention in the past decade. The emphasis now is on helping young students to understand phonemes, the smallest units of sound, and be able to manipulate them in a variety of ways. Research supports that students' awareness of the sounds of spoken words is the best predictor of their success in learning to read. Research also supports that phonemic awareness can be taught and should be embedded in a balanced literacy program, one in which read-alouds, shared reading, interactive writing, and invented spelling are also prevalent.

In this chapter, we focus on teaching phonemic awareness. In Part One, we explain what phonemic awareness is, present what the research has to say, and discuss how to integrate the research results in our teaching. In Part Two, we present teacher-authored, classroom-tested, strategy-based lessons focused on teaching different aspects of phonemic awareness. The chapter concludes with final thoughts and a short list of suggested readings.

Part One: Research Base

What is phonemic awareness?

According to *The Literacy Dictionary*, "Phonemic awareness is the awareness of the sounds (phonemes) that make up spoken words" (Harris & Hodges, 1995, p. 185). Yopp and Yopp extend *The Literacy Dictionary* definition, noting, "Phonemic awareness is the awareness that the speech stream consists of a sequence of sounds—specifically phonemes, the smallest unit of sound that makes a difference in communication" (2000, p. 130). The International Reading Association's position statement on phonemic awareness (1998) notes that phonemic awareness refers to an insight about oral language and the ability to segment and manipulate the sounds of speech. All three sources are careful to note that phonemic awareness is different from phonics, which they generally define as a method that uses the correlation of phonemes (sounds) and graphemes (written letters) to teach reading.

What does the research tell us?

Researchers agree that phonemic awareness is a powerful predictor of reading and spelling acquisition (Ball & Blachman, 1991; Ehri & Nunes, 2002; International Reading Association, 1998). We also know that phonemic awareness can be taught (Snow et al., 1998; Yopp, 1992), but Yopp and Yopp (2000) caution that its instruction needs to be part of a broader reading program in order to be effective.

The National Reading Panel (2000) presents similar conclusions, noting that teaching children to manipulate phonemes in words was highly effective under a variety of teaching conditions with a variety of learners. The panel also concluded that phonemic awareness training results in improved phonemic awareness, reading, and spelling.

Researchers and practitioners agree that phonemic awareness instruction must be naturally situated in the context of a broader literacy program that is linguistically rich. It should be engaging, lively, sensitive to students' needs, and fun. In addition, Yopp and Yopp (2000) note that phonemic awareness instruction should be child-appropriate, deliberate, and purposeful.

Yopp and Yopp (2000) also suggest that when planning phonemic awareness instruction, we should consider

- the unit of sound to be emphasized,
- the type of operation to be performed with the unit,

- whether the activity will be strictly oral—songs, poems, stories, games—or involve concrete cues (manipulatives) such as chips and letters. (Clapping is an auditory cue; blocks or chips are visual cues; jumping when they hear a sound is a kinesthetic cue.)

Yopp and Yopp (2000) note that students do not need to master one area of phonemic awareness before being exposed to others.

The characteristics of phonemic awareness training found to be most effective in enhancing phonemic awareness, reading, and spelling skills include explicitly and systematically teaching children to manipulate phonemes with letters, focusing the instruction on one or two types of phoneme manipulations rather than multiple types, and teaching children in small groups (National Reading Panel, 2000, p. 2-6). The National Reading Panel (2000) suggests that when teaching phonemic awareness, we should keep the following in mind:

- Phonemic awareness instruction does not constitute a complete reading program. Rather, it provides children with essential foundational knowledge in the alphabetic system. It is one necessary instructional component within a complete and integrated reading program. Several additional competencies must be acquired as well to ensure that children will learn to read and write.

- There are many ways to teach phonemic awareness effectively. When teaching phonemic awareness, evaluate the methods against measured success in students.

The motivation of both students and their teachers is a critical ingredient of success. Research has not specifically focused on this.

How can we make the research-teaching connection?

Research indicates that phonemic awareness can and should be taught. Integrating the various aspects of this skill into our teaching will benefit our students. In Part Two of this chapter, we present lessons that focus on phonemic awareness. The lessons feature direct and guided instruction, as well as opportunities for independent application. They incorporate different genres at a variety of levels and provide students with plenty of time to read, write, sketch, and discuss independently. Additional ideas for teaching phonemic awareness can be found in Appendix B (p. 179).

Part Two: Lesson Overview

In this chapter, all of the lessons focus on phonemic awareness. Featured texts include rhymes, songs, and children's books such as *Old MacDonald Had a Woodshop* (Shulman, 2002); *Brown Bear, Brown Bear, What Do You See?* (Martin, 1970); *Panda Bear, Panda Bear, What Do You See?* (Martin, 2003); *We're Going on a Lion Hunt* (Axtell, 1999); *Polar Bear, Polar Bear, What Do You Hear?* (Martin, 1997); *K Is for Kissing a Cool Kangaroo* (Andreae, 2002); *Duck, Duck, Goose! (A Coyote's on the Loose!)* (Beaumont, 2004); *This Is the Teacher* (Greene, 2004); *Wild About Books* (Sierra, 2004); *Barnyard Banter* (Fleming, 1994); and *The Secret Birthday Message* (Carle, 1997).

The lessons in this chapter are appropriate for all different types of learners. In our classrooms we may have students who speak English as a second language, struggling readers, and students with special needs. To accommodate all of these learners, the lessons include the use of multiple modalities (singing, sketching, and so on) working with partners, books on tape, cross-age experiences, and extra guided instruction for students who struggle. For ideas on further adapting the lessons, see "Final Thoughts" at the end of the chapter.

This section features six teacher-authored, classroom-tested lessons that each address a specific aspect of phonemic awareness: phoneme isolation, phoneme identity, phoneme categorization, phoneme blending, phoneme segmentation, and phoneme deletion and addition. The lessons include teacher think-alouds and student work. They were designed using the Guided Comprehension Model for the Primary Grades (McLaughlin, 2003), which was discussed in Chapter 1.

LESSON 1 Phoneme Isolation

Requires recognizing individual sounds in words, for example, I would say, "Tell me the first sound in paste," *and students would respond, "/p/."*   (Ehri & Nunes, 2002, p. 111)

STAGE 1 Teacher-Directed Whole-Group Instruction

SONG/RHYME: Song sung to the tune of "Old MacDonald Had a Farm"

> Old MacDonald had a farm
>
> E-I-E-I-O,
>
> And on his farm he had a pig,
>
> E-I-E-I-O,
>
> With a /p/ /p/ here,
>
> And a /p/ /p/ there,
>
> Here a /p/,
>
> There a /p/,
>
> Everywhere a /p/ /p/,
>
> Old McDonald had a pig,
>
> E-I-E-I-O!

(Change "pig" to different animals: cow, horse, rooster, dog, cat, etc.)

TEXT: *Old MacDonald Had a Woodshop* (Shulman, 2002)

EXPLAIN: I began by explaining that we would be working with the beginning and ending sounds that we had been learning. I said, "I will be reading a book, and we will be singing some songs and doing some activities that will help us recognize individual sounds."

DEMONSTRATE: I began by reading *Old MacDonald Had a Woodshop* to the students. Repeated sounds are stressed throughout the book. The students enjoyed the playful story, and after I had read a page or two, they joined in saying the repeated sounds. When I finished reading, we discussed the story and talked about how much fun the repeated sounds were. I asked, "What sounds do the tools in the workshop make?" Students responded with *swish, swash; squeak, squeak; scritch, scratch; chip, chip; tap, tap; rurr, rurr; zztt, zztt.* When we finished reading, Amelia said, "I was wondering what she was building during the story. It was funny that she built Old MacDonald's farm." Then I demonstrated phoneme isolation by saying some animal names and identifying their beginning sounds (*lizard*, /l/; *bear*, /b/; *fox*, /f/; *monkey*, /m/; etc.). The students seemed to pick up on this quickly; when I provided different animals, they all wanted to isolate the beginning sound.

GUIDE: I organized the students in pairs and gave each pair a set of animal picture cards. One partner was to show the animal card and the other was to say the name of the animal and then isolate its beginning sound. To challenge some of the students, I had them switch roles and try to tell the sound the animal name ended with. For example, Wilson showed Abigail a picture of a duck and she said, "*Duck* ends in /k/." Abigail showed Wilson a picture of a cat and he said, "*Cat* ends in /t/." This was a little harder for the students, but it proved to be a good challenge for some of them. Some of the animal picture cards I used were deer, lion, rabbit, mouse, cat, tiger, camel, and turtle. I made the picture cards by cutting out photos of animals from magazines and gluing them to 4 x 6 inch index cards.

PRACTICE: I hung a poster of the familiar song "Old MacDonald Had a Farm" on the easel. We practiced singing it together and I pointed at the words as we sang. Then I told the students that I was going to change the kind of animal to a different one each time we sang the song. I explained that they would need to decide what sound each animal name begins with. We sang the song using *cow, horse, pig, rooster, dog,* and *cat*. These are the lyrics we sang using the word *cow*:

> Old MacDonald had a farm,
> E-I-E-I-O,
> And on his farm he had a cow,
> E-I-E-I-O,
> With a /c/ /c/ here,
> And a /c/ /c/ there,
> Here a /c/,
> There a /c/,
> Everywhere a /c/ /c/,
> Old MacDonald had a cow,
> E-I-E-I-O

REFLECT: The students were very successful in isolating the beginning sounds in the animal names. They all agreed it was much harder when we tried to do the ending sounds, so we decided that was something we needed to work on.

STAGE 2 Teacher-Guided Small-Group Instruction

SONG/RHYME: Sung to the tune of "London Bridge Is Falling Down"

(Teacher verse)	(Student response)
What's the last sound that you hear?	/t/ is the sound that I hear,
That you hear, that you hear	That I hear, that I hear
What's the last sound that you hear	/t/ is the sound that I hear
In *cat*, *cat*, *cat*?	at the end of *cat*.

REVIEW: I began by reviewing our consonant letter sounds. I used letter cards to review the sounds we had been working on. Then I reminded the group of the song we had sung earlier with the whole class. I said to the students, "You did such a great job with the beginning sounds that we are ready to work on the ending sounds." They all remembered that identifying the last sound was a bit more challenging.

GUIDE: I held up some picture cards of various objects for the group and had the students isolate the ending sound for each picture. For example, I held up a picture card of a kite and Joelle said, "*Kite* ends in /t/." After the group responded to various pictures, I introduced a new song in which we would need to figure out the ending sounds. I told them the tune of the song was "London Bridge Is Falling Down." We sang the original song to remind us of the tune. Next, I sang the teacher's verse to the children and taught them how to respond. I used the word *cat* for the example. I asked the students, "What ending sound does *cat* make?" They all responded with /t/. Then I taught the students the lyrics that they would respond with. We sang the song using different words from more picture cards. The words that we used were *ball*, *purse*, *feet*, *desk*, *pen*, and *door*.

PRACTICE: After singing the song, I wanted to see how individual students could apply what we had been practicing. I pulled various picture cards and asked students to respond with either the beginning or ending sound. Some of the picture cards I used showed a hose, tree, candle, stapler, kite, and pig.

REFLECT: Working in this small group setting helped me to identify the students who were successfully isolating beginning and ending sounds and those who needed additional instruction. Many of the students still agreed that isolating ending sounds was harder, so we decided to continue to work on those in small groups, in centers, and at home.

Student-Facilitated Centers

ABC CENTER: Students had six little brown lunch sacks with a picture and sound printed on the front (/t/, /l/, /r/, /m/, /d/, and /n/). These were sounds we had recently practiced, but any letter sounds could have been used. At the center, I placed numerous picture cards that represented these beginning sounds. Students put the picture cards into the correct letter sound bag. Then they selected one of the letter bags and drew on a piece of paper the letter sound that they had chosen and the objects they had put into that bag. The students who were comfortable isolating ending sounds practiced by using ending sounds in a similar activity. Figure 2-1 shows the sound Raoul selected and the objects he drew. I labeled his drawing.

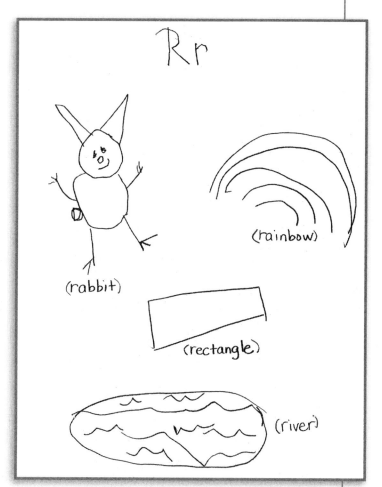

FIGURE 2-1

FIGURE 2-2

LISTENING CENTER: Students listened to *Dr. Seuss's ABC* (Seuss, 1996). In this book, each letter of the alphabet is presented along with a sentence in which nearly all of the words begin with the targeted letter. When students finished listening to the book, they took a paper that had four pictures drawn down the left side. They drew a picture of another word that began with the same sound as the picture on the left. The pictures that I drew down the first side were a cat, a flag, a ring, and a monkey. Mai's completed work appears in Figure 2-2.

(**STAGE 3**)   Teacher-Facilitated Whole-Group Reflection

SHARE: Students shared their center papers with the class. Some also said a word and the class responded by isolating the beginning and ending sounds.

REFLECT: We reflected on the different songs and activities we had participated in during our lesson. Many of the students commented that they enjoyed the listening center and would like to listen to other ABC books. They also thought we should continue working on our beginning and ending sounds.

SET NEW GOALS: Students decided we should continue working on our beginning and ending sounds in small groups. For homework, students drew two objects that started with the letter sounds that we had been practicing. Students who needed additional help with isolating their sounds would work with our classroom aide or me.

Assessment Options

To assess the students, I used observation and their completed center papers at the ABC and Listening Centers. When I was observing, I listened carefully to the sounds the students provided. At the ABC and Listening Centers, I reviewed the objects that were drawn.

LESSON 2   Phoneme Identity

Requires recognizing the common sound in different words, for example, "Tell me the sound that is the same in bike, boy, *and* bell." *(/b/)*   (Ehri & Nunes, 2002, p. 111)

STAGE 1   Teacher-Directed Whole-Group Instruction

TEXTS: *Brown Bear, Brown Bear, What Do You See?* (Martin, 1970)

Panda Bear, Panda Bear, What Do You See? (Martin, 2003)

EXPLAIN: I explained to the students that we would be working with our beginning sounds as we read the story *Brown Bear, Brown Bear, What Do You See?* Our focus for the day would be to decide what beginning sound each set of words contained. I said, "Today we will write a class story telling what might happen after Bill Martin's story ends. We will use our beginning sounds."

DEMONSTRATE: Before reading the story to the students, I wanted to make sure that they could identify the beginning sound in sets of words that began with the same sound. I used the example of: *cat, couch,* and *cap.* The students responded with /c/. I did a few more examples with the students to make sure they were able to identify the beginning sounds.

GUIDE: I began reading aloud to the class *Brown Bear, Brown Bear, What Do You See?* After reading each new page, I would stop and have them identify what sound was the same as the color name (*brown, bear,* /b/). I did this throughout the book. The students were successful in identifying all of the beginning sounds.

PRACTICE: After reading the story with the class, I asked students to help me write a sequel to *Brown Bear, Brown Bear, What Do You See?* I explained that I would give them each a color name and they would need to come up with an animal name that starts with the same beginning sound. Here are some of their examples: Red rooster, red rooster; Orange octopus, orange octopus; Yellow yak, yellow yak; Green gator, green gator; Blue bull, blue bull; Purple penguin, purple penguin; Black bat, black bat; Brown beaver, brown beaver; Pink pig, pink pig; White whale, white whale.

Next, students illustrated their favorite animal or created a new one to illustrate. I hung their pictures on a bulletin board to help them with their beginning-sound recognition. Figure 2-3 shows Melanie's and Riccardo's drawings.

FIGURE 2-3

REFLECT: We reflected on the importance of knowing our beginning sounds to help us with our reading and writing. The students really enjoyed coming up with new animals to put into our sequel.

STAGE 2 Teacher-Guided Small-Group Instruction

SONG/ RHYME: Sung as a march or military cadence (Fredericks, 2001)

Students:	There's a sound that's in my ear.
Teacher:	What's the first sound you can hear?
Students:	Tell us some words one, two, three.
Teacher:	Then you must listen carefully: bake, bail, bank.
Students:	/b/

Students:	There's a sound that's in my ear.
Teacher:	What's the first sound you can hear?
Students:	Tell us some words one, two, three.
Teacher:	Then you must listen carefully: girl, goose, get.
Students:	/g/

REVIEW: I reminded students about how we identified the beginning sound in a set of words. To refresh their memories, I told them some of the colored animals we had come up with earlier. I gave the students a few sets of words and they identified the beginning sound (*dog, door, dance*: /d/).

GUIDE: Then I introduced the song, which was written on a chart on my easel. I taught the students their part and then gave them three new words. We sang the song a few times, changing the words each time. Some of the students wanted to sing the teacher part. They gave the group three words that all started with the same sound and the rest of us responded with the beginning sound. Keisha said, "Ball, bat, and bear." Ryan told the class that the words Keisha had said all started with /b/.

PRACTICE: I provided the students with papers, and each paper had the symbol of a letter sound on the top of the page. They had to draw three objects that started with their sound. If they finished and wanted a challenge, I had them try to write the sounds they heard in the names of the objects they drew. If they finished that, some of them turned their paper over and practiced doing the same thing with a different letter. Figure 2-4 shows Leilani's completed work. She had the letter sound /p/ on top of her paper. She drew pictures of a pig, a plane, and a purse. I labeled her drawings.

REFLECT: Students shared their pictures of their three objects that started with the same letter sound. The students enjoyed the song and asked later if we could sing it again.

FIGURE 2-4

Student-Facilitated Centers

ABC CENTER: To practice working with their sounds, the students played a memory game with a partner. They used picture cards that I had preselected (only two cards had the same beginning sound). Each student drew two cards. If their cards began with the same sound, they got to keep the cards. The students also needed to tell their partners what sound the picture cards started with. They could discuss whether they agreed with each other. To provide a way for the students to check their answers at the end of the game, I had drawn the matches on a piece of paper. The students checked this sheet to see if their matches were correct. The person with the most matches won the game.

LISTENING CENTER: To practice their sounds at the Listening Center, students each received a paper that contained boxes numbered one through ten. I prerecorded myself saying ten different sets of three words. The words I used were *girl, goat, geese; boat, boy, bear; kite, kid, kangaroo; love, lid, lunch; turtle, table, turn; cat, couch, car; dog, dove, dish; fish, fire, film; horse, hair, hill;* and *jack, jump, jelly.* As they heard each set of words, they wrote its beginning sound in the appropriate box, sequentially. If students finished early, they could write a letter sound on the back of their paper and draw three pictures that started with the same sound. Students had done this earlier in small groups, so they understood the directions.

STAGE 3   Teacher-Facilitated Whole-Group Reflection

SHARE: Students shared their colorful animals from the whole-group lesson and we hung the animals on a bulletin board. Then students shared the work they had done at the centers.

REFLECT: We reflected on the importance of knowing our beginning sounds to help us in our daily writing. Many of the students wanted to sing the march song again as a whole group, so we sang it a few times to review. At the end of our lesson, I read *Panda Bear, Panda Bear, What Do You See?* to the students. We discussed the animals in the story and their beginning sounds.

SET NEW GOALS: The students did a great job recognizing the common sounds in different words. Next, they wanted the challenge of identifying a sound that did not belong in the set.

Assessment Options

I used a variety of assessments, including observation, animal drawings, and the Listening Center letter identification paper. To observe, I listened carefully to the students' responses in each of the stages of the lesson. I checked the students' letter-sound responses on their drawings and at the Listening Center to make sure they had the correct letter sound or pictures for the letter sound they had chosen.

LESSON 3   Phoneme Categorization

Requires recognizing the word with the odd sound in a sequence of three or four words, for example, "Which word does not belong: bus, bun, or rug?" (rug)

(Ehri & Nunes, 2002, p. 111)

STAGE 1   Teacher-Directed Whole-Group Instruction

TEXT/SONG: *We're Going on a Lion Hunt* (Axtell, 1999)

"We're Going on a Mystery Trip"—sung as an echo or repeating song (adapted from "We're Going on a Bear Hunt")

EXPLAIN: I began by reading aloud *We're Going on a Lion Hunt* (Axtell, 1999) and discussing it with the students. Then I explained that we were going to go on a mystery trip today and we had to pack our suitcase. I said, "I have some items that we need to pack, but not all of them will fit into the suitcase." I actually brought in an old suitcase for our trip. I asked the students for their help in packing my suitcase because I wasn't sure what items I could bring. I told the students that they needed to decide which item in each group we couldn't bring by listening carefully to the beginning sounds of the items. I said, "The item that begins with a sound that is different from the sounds that the other items begin with is the one that cannot be packed in our suitcase."

DEMONSTRATE: I demonstrated by giving the students a few examples of the items I might want to pack. The first example I gave was "coat, fish, and cat." I thought aloud about the sounds I heard at the beginning of each items. I said, "*Fish* does not belong because it starts with a /f/ instead of /c/ like the other two items." I gave another example and thought aloud about "cup, socks, and soap." I said, "*Cup* does not begin with /s/ like *socks* and *soap* do, so I will not pack the cup."

GUIDE: I guided the students through a few examples of their own before I taught them the song we were going to sing. Our first example was "cat, cup, rug." Some of the student examples were "hat, brush, and banana" and "toothpaste, turtle, and rabbit." After they successfully identified which items would not be packed, I taught the students the lyrics to the song "We're Going on a Mystery Trip." I told the students to repeat after me and that at the end of the song they would need to decide which item would not be packed in our suitcase. We sang the song five or six times, using different object names each time. Some examples of the words we used were *socks, snake,* and *frog; ring, glasses,* and *gum;* and *peaches, lamp,* and *pig.* In these sequences, the students correctly identified frog, ring and lamp as the items we would not pack in the suitcase.

"We're Going on a Mystery Trip"

Teacher:	We're going on a mystery trip.
Students:	We're going on a mystery trip.
Teacher:	What are we going to pack?
Students:	What are we going to pack?
Teacher:	A cat, cap, and rug.
Students:	A cat, cap, and rug.
Teacher:	But only two of these things can fit.
Students:	Only two of these things can fit.
Teacher:	Which one doesn't belong?
Students:	Which one doesn't belong?
Students:	Rug.

PRACTICE: The students returned to their desks to practice on their own. Each student received a picture of a closet. The students were to listen to the objects that I named, decide which item we could not pack in the suitcase, and draw a picture of that item in the closet. The items in the closet were the items that would stay at home. I gave them three sets of objects to respond to: "clock, cat, and dog"; "tree, horse, and hat"; "book, fish, and butterfly." Then I collected and reviewed their papers to see which students still needed extra help identifying the sound that didn't belong.

REFLECT: We reflected on the fact that we had to be careful listeners to decide which sound didn't belong. We discussed that we should say the words quietly to ourselves to see which word moved our mouth differently. Shanda asked, "Where are we going with all of these strange items in our suitcase?" That led to our writing a class story, which the students illustrated and I recorded and read aloud. Figure 2-5 shows our completed story.

We are going on a mystery trip. We will take a <u>clock</u>, so we will know what time it is. We will take a <u>book</u>, so we can read before we go to sleep. On the way, we will see a <u>cat</u> and a <u>horse</u> wearing a funny <u>hat</u>. A <u>butterfly</u> will fly around a flower. We will take our mystery trip in the summer, and when we arrive we will swim in a lake.

FIGURE 2-5

⬭ STAGE 2 ⬭ Teacher-Guided Small-Group Instruction

TEXT: *Each Peach Pear Plum* (Ahlberg & Ahlberg, 1978)

REVIEW: I reviewed by giving the students a few more three-word examples (*feet, fish,* and *cow; hand, nose,* and *hip*). They told me which word did not belong (*cow, nose*). I then said, "We will be reading an I Spy book and in it you will need to try to find many famous story characters." I reminded them that they would also need to identify on each page which word did not begin with the same sound as the other two words.

GUIDE: I read the students the title of the book *Each Peach Pear Plum.* I asked them, of the four words in the title which word did not start with the same sound as all the other words. They all agreed that the word *each* did not belong. I read them the story, stopping for the students to find the missing character and also to identify the word that did not begin with the same sound. Some examples I used throughout the text were *pear, plum, Tom; spy, Jack, Jill; safe, dry, spy; spy, stairs, three.* There are many choices to choose from; I chose just three on each page. The students did a wonderful job identifying the word that did not belong.

PRACTICE: After we finished reading the story, we played a game to practice identifying the sound that didn't belong. I gave each student in the group three index cards. Each child had index cards labeled 1, 2, and 3. They laid out their cards in front of them in numerical order. Next, I asked the students to choose which word did not belong and to hold up their card to indicate whether it was the first, second, or third word. I demonstrated how to hold up the cards after I said a set of words. The example I used was *kangaroo, kite, lion.* Then I held up the third card because *lion* starts with /l/ and the other words start with /k/. The students then held up their cards to the different word sets <u>bear</u>, *apple, ax; dog, dish, <u>boy</u>; rabbit, <u>cat</u>, rake; candle, cup, <u>dish</u>; lake, <u>river</u>, lamb; <u>girl</u>, bat, ball.* The students were able to identify almost all of the words that should not be in the sets. I noted the students who exhibited any difficulty, so I could spend additional time working with them later.

REFLECT: The students shared their thoughts on the book *Each Peach Pear Plum*. Many of the students liked the book because they felt it was like a game when they were listening to the story. They liked finding the characters and guessing the word that didn't belong. The students also commented on the game. They thought it was harder to try to figure out the number of the word that did not belong, but most of them were successful in doing so.

Student-Facilitated Centers

LISTENING CENTER: Each student received a paper that had the numbers one through eight in boxes. I prerecorded myself saying eight different sets of three words. Students drew a picture of the word that did not belong in that group in the correct numbered box. The examples I used were *dog, dish, cat*; *ball, horse, hat*; *rose, fish, rabbit*; *square, rock, star*; *computer, book, can*; *head, window, whale*; *kite, nose, nickel*; *dime, door, flower*. I spoke very slowly on the tape and repeated the words three times each. Students put their completed work in their reading folders and shared them in Stage 3 of our lesson. Grace's completed work appears in Figure 2-6.

FIGURE 2-6

TEACHER CENTER: Students were assigned partners that were at similar levels to work at the Teacher Center. I had made several transparencies that had four pictures on them. Three of the pictures began with the same sound, but one did not. I placed these in the Teacher Center, which already contained an overhead projector (that I kept on the floor) and a miniature paper screen (that I had taped to the wall). The partner who was playing the student placed the transparency on the overhead projector. Then he said what each picture was and used a transparency marker to circle the picture that didn't start with the same sound as the other pictures. The student playing the teacher either agreed or disagreed. The "student" and "teacher" alternated their roles. Figure 2-7 shows an example of Glenn and Karen's completed work from the Teacher Center.

FIGURE 2-7

SHARE: Students shared the pictures of their closets and what they had put in them and the work they had completed at their centers. Then pairs of students drew groups of three objects, "read" them, and asked the class which one did not belong. We had a fun time explaining which objects did not belong, and the students seemed quite confident when responding.

REFLECT: Students shared their thoughts on the fact that the more they practiced, the easier it became to identify the word or object that did not belong in the set. Tim, one of the students, said what had helped him the most was to say the words quietly to himself to see which word made his mouth move differently. Many of the students enjoyed packing the suitcase and wanted to talk more about where they could go with the items.

SET NEW GOALS: Students felt pretty comfortable with identifying the odd sound in the sequence. They wanted me to try giving them more words in the sequence to make it more challenging. I then told the students that our next step would be to try and identify more sounds in various words in order to be able to identify the whole word.

Assessment Options

To assess students, I used a variety of measures, including observation, partner assessment, Listening Center sound identification, and drawings of their closets. To observe, I listened carefully to the students' responses throughout the various stages of the lesson. At the Teacher Center, we used peer assessment. The students made sure their partners had correctly chosen the picture that did not belong. I checked the students' Listening Center sound identification papers to see if the students identified and drew the picture that did not belong. I also made sure students had drawn the correct pictures in their closets.

LESSON 4 · Phoneme Blending

Requires listening to a sequence of separately spoken sounds and combining them to form a recognizable word, for example, "What word is /s/ /k/ /u/ /l/?" (school)

(Ehri & Nunes, 2002, p. 112)

STAGE 1 · Teacher-Directed Whole-Group Instruction

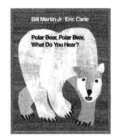

TEXT/SONG: *"The Wheels on the Bus"*

Polar Bear, Polar Bear, What Do You Hear? (Martin, 1997)

EXPLAIN: I explained to the students that today they would be blending letters together to form words. To help the students understand what it meant to blend sounds together, I brought in a plastic mixing bowl and spoon. I told them that when we blend sounds together it is like mixing the ingredients together when we cook. I explained that instead of mixing ingredients, we were going to mix letter-sounds together. Then I took out my letter cards to help them visualize what we were going to be doing.

DEMONSTRATE: To demonstrate, I said the sounds /c/, /a/, and /t/ and asked the students what the letter sounds sounded like when I said them in order. The students responded with the word *cat*. Then I repeated the same process with the words *dot, hop*, and *bit*. Each time the students responded with the correct word.

GUIDE: I guided the students as a group to try blending sounds to make a few more words. I said the letter-sounds for the words *cap, dog*, and *hit* and the students blended them correctly. Next, I taught the students a song that is sung to the tune of "The Wheels on the Bus." We sang the first verse of "The Wheels on the Bus" to remind ourselves of the tune. Then I sang the song using the word *cat*. The lyrics were:

The sounds in the word go /c/ /a/ /t/; /c/ /a/ /t/; /c/ /a/ /t/.

The sounds in the word go /c/ /a/ /t/,

Can you guess the word? Cat!

They were all able to say the word and enjoyed singing it. Next, I sang the song segmenting other three-letter words—*sun, pig, red, fun, tan, fan, run*, and *hot*, and the students responded by saying the words. Then I tried some harder words. I used *school*, *spider*, *jump*, *desk*, and *pencil* and the students blended the sounds and sang the correct word each time.

PRACTICE: The students returned to their desks to practice blending sounds together. This time I said an animal name segmented into its sounds and the students guessed which animal I was saying. I used the words /l/ /i/ /on/, /b/ /ir/ /d/, /f/ /r/ /o/ /g/, /p/ /i/ /g/, /t/ /ur/ /t/ /l/, and /f/ /i/ /sh/. To complete our lesson, I read aloud *Polar Bear, Polar Bear, What Do You Hear?* This time instead of reading all of the animals' names, I read those that were more difficult and segmented some of the names that were easier, such as sea lion, red wolf, and green sea turtle.

REFLECT: We reflected that we needed to blend the sounds together in the order in which we hear them in order to make a word. I demonstrated again with the mixing bowl to give the students a visual focus, and we did a few more examples together. The students commented on how they enjoyed guessing the words, and Michael, one of my students, said, "I noticed that words all have sounds inside them."

(STAGE 2) Teacher-Guided Small-Group Instruction

TEXTS/SONG: Sung to the tune of "Row, Row, Row Your Boat" (Fredericks, 2001)

K Is for Kissing a Cool Kangaroo (Andreae, 2002)

Duck, Duck, Goose! (A Coyote's on the Loose!) (Beaumont, 2004)

This Is the Teacher (Greene, 2004)

Wild About Books (Sierra, 2004)

REVIEW: We reviewed how to blend the sounds in the order in which we hear them, and did a few examples together. This time we used *rock*, *time*, *hand*, and *book*. Then I read aloud *K Is for Kissing a Cool Kangaroo*. After discussing it with the students, I read it a second time and segmented the rhyming words. The students readily blended the sounds and provided the words.

GUIDE: The students seemed to be comfortable blending the sounds together, so I taught them a song sung to the tune of "Row, Row, Row Your Boat." We sang the original lyrics of the song together first to ensure that everyone recognized the tune. Then I sang the song with different lyrics and asked the students to sing the blended sounds. The lyrics were

> Say, say, say the sounds
>
> Gently in a row
>
> Slowly, slowly, slowly, slowly
>
> [Teacher says:] /d/ /u/ /ck/
>
> [Children say:] duck

The words I used were *duck*, *sheep*, *chair*, *food*, *time*, *flower*, and *pencil*. The students were able to successfully blend the sounds to make the words every time.

PRACTICE: To practice, the students worked with partners to respond when I said the letter sounds of more animal names. After they guessed each animal, the pair said a sentence telling something about the animal. When we finished, students drew pictures of their favorite animals and told their partners something about them.

REFLECT: The students shared that they liked blending sounds to make words, and they liked sharing information about animals. I explained that we can blend sounds to form all kinds of words, not just the words we know. I also explained that the more we practiced blending our sounds, the easier it would become. Then the students whispered words to me and I segmented the sounds while they and their classmates guessed the words.

Student-Facilitated Center and Routine

LISTENING CENTER: Students used a tape recorder to listen to an audiotape of animal riddles that I had prerecorded. The students each had a paper folded into six boxes, which were numbered 1–6. In response to each riddle they drew the animal in the correct box.

The riddles that I used were

1. I'm thinking of an animal that likes to fetch things. It is a /d/ /o/ /g/.

2. I'm thinking of an animal that sleeps a lot. It is a /c/ /a/ /t/.

3. I'm thinking of an animal that lives in water. It is a /f/ /i/ /sh/.

4. I'm thinking of an animal that likes to sing. It is a /b/ /ir/ /d/.

5. I'm thinking of an animal that likes to hop. It is a /r/ /a/ /b/ /i/ /t/.

6. I'm thinking of an animal that roars loudly. It is a /l/ /i/ /on/.

Figure 2-8 shows Alice's completed response.

FIGURE 2-8

CROSS-AGE READING EXPERIENCES: All of the students have reading buddies from third grade that come and help them occasionally with their reading. In this case, I had met with the third-grade buddies and given them a list of words in which the sounds were segmented. I explained that they needed to have their buddies blend the sounds to form words and I provided them with many examples. The cross-age reading experiences began with the third graders reading predictable rhyming texts aloud and discussing the books with their buddies. Books they read included *This Is the Teacher*; *Wild About Books*; and *Duck, Duck, Goose*. Then the third graders segmented a number of words for the students to blend together and kept track of the words students blended successfully and unsuccessfully. The words I had segmented on the buddy lists were: *cab*, *fish*, *trip*, *sad*, *gum*, *fire*, *lake*, *rabbit*, *shade*, and *lamp*. If the students had any difficulty, the third graders had other examples to use with them.

STAGE 3   Teacher-Facilitated Whole-Group Reflection

SHARE: Students shared their center riddles, and some had made up new ones for us to guess. Then we discussed their cross-age reading experiences, and, as always, the students reported how much they enjoyed learning with their third-grade buddies. They seemed to enjoy blending the sounds the third graders provided and felt they were quite proficient at it.

REFLECT: We reflected on the importance of blending sounds to help us learn how to read and write. Then we all sang "Row, Row, Row Your Boat" using some different words.

SET NEW GOALS: We decided we still needed lots of work on blending sounds to form words, so we decided to continue doing lots of blending activities.

Assessment Options

I used a variety of assessments, including observation, riddle drawings, and reading buddy assessing of the blended words. I observed throughout the various stages of the lesson by listening carefully to the students' responses. I checked to make sure that the students drew the correct animal as I blended the animal names. The reading buddies assessed their partners as they practiced blending words. If a student was having difficulty, the buddy helped the student and reported his or her findings back to me.

LESSON 5 Phoneme Segmentation

Requires breaking a word into sounds by tapping out or counting the sounds, or by pronouncing and positioning a marker for each sound, for example, "How many phonemes in ship?" (three: /š/ /ĭ/ /p/) (Ehri & Nunes, 2002, p. 112)

STAGE 1 Teacher-Directed Whole-Group Instruction

RHYME: "The Cat and the Fiddle"

Hey, diddle, diddle,

The cat and the fiddle,

The cow jumped

Over the moon.

The little dog laughed

To see such a sport,

And the dish ran away with the spoon.

EXPLAIN: I said to students, "We will be breaking words into the sounds we hear. We have already taken sounds and blended them into words. This time we are going to start with the word first and figure out what sounds make up the word." I used my picture cards. I showed the students the picture of the cat and I said, "Cat." I said, "We need to figure out the sounds in *cat*."

DEMONSTRATE: To demonstrate, I said *cat* again, but this time I said it slowly, exaggerating the sounds. Then I thought aloud. I said, "When I said *cat*, I heard three sounds. I heard /c/ /a/ /t/. So I think *cat* is made up of three sounds and they are /c/ /a/ /t/." I tried a few more examples. I used all three-letter words, so that it would be easier for the students to hear the individual sounds. I used *dog*, *jet*, and *top*. By the time I finished *dog*, they were volunteering the sounds. Then I showed the students the word *fish*. When I tried to break up the sounds in *fish*, I told them that my mouth wouldn't let me break up the /sh/. I explained that sometimes we can't break up all of the sounds, so we keep them together as one sound. Then we tried the word *chin*. We decided that /ch/ should stay together. The students helped me break up the word into the sounds /ch/ /i/ /n/. I pointed out that even though the word *chin* has four letters, we only broke it up into three sounds. Then we said *chin* together and segmented its phonemes again.

GUIDE: To guide the students, I explained that we were going to practice together breaking words into the sounds by reading a nursery rhyme. I read the nursery rhyme "The Cat and the Fiddle" and the students chose words for us to segment. Words they selected included *fiddle*, *sport*, and *dish*. Each time I asked the students to say the word with me and count the sounds they heard. Every time we heard a sound, we put a token in the center of the table. Then we said the sounds we heard.

PRACTICE: To practice, we sat on the floor around a taped rectangle that was split into four sections. I demonstrated by showing how we would jump into a different section each time we heard a different sound in a word. I said, "We will count how many sounds we hear in each word, by counting the sections we have jumped." The first word I demonstrated was *hop*. To demonstrate, I jumped into the first section as I said "/h/." Next, I jumped into the following section as I said "/o/." Finally, I jumped into the third section as I said "/p/." Then we counted the number of sections I had jumped to. We decided I had jumped into three sections, so *hop* must have three sounds. The students volunteered to jump to count the sounds in *rag, jet, ham, bat, rest, bag, shop,* and *lunch*. Although only some students actually got to hop in the rectangle, all of the students were saying the different sounds and telling the number of sounds we heard. I continued having the children volunteer to do the jumping as we segmented words for the next few days. The students liked this activity and I knew we would use it again in the future.

REFLECT: To reflect, we reviewed how we broke up the word into the different sounds we heard. Lionel observed that it was helpful to clap as he said each sound in his head. I told the students that we would try his method later in the day.

(STAGE 2) Teacher-Guided Small-Group Instruction

TEXT: *Barnyard Banter* (Fleming, 1994)

REVIEW: To review, the students segmented a few words into the sounds they heard. I used the words *cup*, *dad*, and *mom*. We tried the clapping method to help us count the sounds. Many students agreed that it was helpful. I introduced the story *Barnyard Banter*. Then I said, "I will stop at different points in the story, so you can break up some animal names into sounds."

GUIDE: Before I began to read the story, I gave each student a piece of paper that had four boxes in a row on it. The paper looked like the rectangle they saw earlier on the floor. I gave them each four M&Ms. I explained that they were going to use the M&Ms to help them count the sounds. For each sound that they heard, they placed an M&M into a box. I demonstrated with the word *bug*. We decided *bug* had three sounds, so we placed an M&M in each of the first three boxes. Then I read the story, stopping at various animal words I thought the students could segment. I stopped numerous times. Here are some examples I used: *moo* (2), *pig* (3), *duck* (3), *mice* (3), *hen* (3), *pond* (4), *goose* (3), and *squeak* (4). Any words in the story could be used; these were just some that I chose. The students responded successfully and enjoyed learning with manipulatives they could eat at the end of the lesson.

PRACTICE: I gave the students more words to practice in their boxes. Then I passed out rhythm sticks to each child. I gave them some words and they tapped out the number of sounds they heard in each word. We used our rhythm sticks to tap out the words *pin*, *tap*, *fun*, *sun*, *cap*, *rip*, *pop*, and *book*.

REFLECT: We reflected on the different ways we could figure out how many sounds we were hearing in words. Many of the students enjoyed the jumping best, but they also liked moving the M&Ms into the boxes because they could eat the M&Ms when they were finished. Jeffrey said, "I like jumping, clapping, and the M&Ms. They help me to hear the sounds. I didn't know all the sounds were in there before."

Student-Facilitated Centers

ABC CENTER: I gave the students charts that had the numbers 2, 3, and 4 at the top. I also provided picture cards of various items. Students worked with partners to place the picture cards under the correct number of sounds in the word. The picture cards included pictures of a bee, dog, hen, sheep, flag, tree, stick, plane, hat, and ball. When they finished, they drew on their paper one object for each column—two sounds, three sounds, and four sounds. Figure 2-9 shows what Kanisha drew in her sound columns.

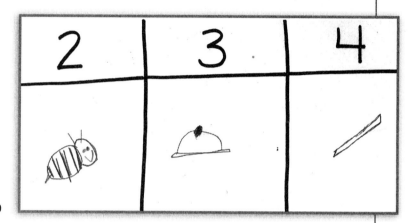

FIGURE 2-9

LISTENING CENTER: I provided students with pieces of paper with the numbers 1 through 10 written in boxes. They listened to the tape, on which I had prerecorded ten words. As the students listened, they focused on the number of sounds they heard in each word and wrote the number in the correct box. The students were able to use the rhythm sticks or clap to help themselves figure out how many sounds they heard.

(**STAGE 3**) Teacher-Facilitated Whole-Group Reflection

SHARE: Students shared their work from the centers and said words to partners who clapped the number of sounds they heard. For example, Seimus said, "How many sounds do you hear in the word *desk*?" Maggie responded, "I hear four sounds: /d/ /e/ /s/ /k/."

REFLECT: Students reflected on which method was easiest for them to use to figure out the number of sounds they were hearing. Most agreed that clapping or tapping was the easiest to do quietly at their desks, but they enjoyed hopping and moving the M&Ms best.

SET NEW GOALS: Some students thought it was hard to decide which sounds stayed together in words such as *shark* and *catch*. So we decided to continue working on segmenting, focusing on more challenging words.

Assessment Options

I used observation to assess the students, as well as reviewing their ABC and Listening Center papers. I checked to make sure the students had drawn a correct picture under the various sound columns at the ABC Center. At the Listening Center, I made sure the students had written the correct number of sounds they heard in each word. If students had difficulty on any of the activities, I continued working with them in small groups.

LESSON 6   Phoneme Deletion and Addition

Phoneme Deletion: *Requires stating the sounds that remain when a specified phoneme is removed, for example, "What is* smile *without the /s/? (*mile*)*

Phoneme Addition: *Adding a sound to a word after a sound has been deleted. For example, "What sound can we add to* at *to make a word meaning something that is worn on someone's head?" (*hat*)*   (Ehri & Nunes, 2002, p. 112)

STAGE 1   Teacher-Directed Whole-Group Instruction

TEXT/SONG: *The Secret Birthday Message* (Carle, 1997)

EXPLAIN: I began by explaining to the students that we would be removing sounds from words and adding new sounds to form new words. For example, I asked them, "What is *cat* without the /c/?" The students responded with *at*. Then I asked them what *at* would be if we added /h/ to the beginning. They all said *hat*.

DEMONSTRATE: I began my demonstration by reading aloud to the students. The book I selected was Eric Carle's *The Secret Birthday Message*. When we were making our final predictions, the children were predicting what the surprise would be. It was a dog. After discussing the story with the students, I used the word *dog* to demonstrate phoneme deletion and phoneme addition. I said, "If we take the beginning sound /d/ away from *dog*, we are left with *og*. We can change that into a new word if we add a new beginning sound. So, if we add /f/, our new word is *fog*; if we add /h/, our new word is *hog*." We talked about the meanings of *fog* and *hog*, then I continued to demonstrate using other examples. These included:

What is *hat* without the /h/? (*at*)

What is *at* if we add /m/ to the beginning? (*mat*)

What if we add /s/ to *at*? (*sat*)

GUIDE: I guided students by explaining that we would be doing two things: taking away beginning sounds and adding new sounds to make new words. I said, "When we took /h/ away from *hat*, *at* was left. When we added /m/, we made a new word, *mat*. That's what we're going to do with *seat*, *late*, and *fall*." I reminded the students that we needed to do two things: take away the beginning sound and add a new sound to make a new word.

Then I said, "What is *seat* without the /s/?" The students replied, "*eat*."

I said, "What if we add /n/ to the beginning?" They replied, "*neat*."

I said, "What if we add /m/ to the beginning?" They replied, "*meat*."

We continued talking about the words and deleting and adding phonemes. When we deleted /l/ from *late*, we made the new words *date*, *gate*, *mate*, and *rate*. When we deleted /f/ from *fall*, we made the new words *ball*, *call*, *hall*, and *mall*.

PRACTICE: Next, I explained to the students that I was going to say two words and in the second word I would have changed the beginning, middle, or ending sound. I said, "We are going to need to figure out which sound I changed. If it is the beginning sound, we will touch our heads. If it is the middle sound, we will touch our hips. If it is the ending sound, we will touch our toes." I demonstrated the first one for them. I said, "*Hot* and *hop*." I told the students that I changed the ending sound from /t/ to /p/, so I touched my toes. They all agreed. Next, the students stood up and we practiced touching our heads, hips, and toes. Then we tried the next set of words: *fan* and *ran*. Almost all of the students touched their heads. I reminded them that we were touching our heads for the beginning sound, hips for middle, and toes for the ending sound. I continued with the following sets of words: *hat/hot*, *bat/pat*, *zip/tip*, *can/fan*, *sick/sack*, *ran/rat*, *sing/song*, *miss/kiss*, *walk/talk*, *pig/pit*, and *fun/fin*. Most of the students were able to identify which sound I changed. I noted the few students who were having difficulties and worked with them in small groups later in the day.

REFLECT: We reflected on how we can take away one sound and change the whole word. We also discussed the importance of being able to change a word by changing only one sound. I reminded the students that we can make a lot of new words by changing just one sound. I gave them the example of the word *at* and explained that if we added different beginning sounds to *at*, we could make the words *bat, cat, rat, sat, fat, hat, mat, pat*, and so on. Joseph, one of my students, said, "When we change just the beginning sound, the words rhyme."

(STAGE 2) Teacher-Guided Small-Group Instruction

REVIEW: We reviewed by discussing the importance of being able to take away sounds from words and add new sounds to form new words.

GUIDE: Then we did a few more examples. These included:

What is *gate* without the /g/? (*ate*)

What is *ate* if we add /l/? (*late*)

What is *fit* without the /f/? (*it*)

What is *it* if we add /s/? (*sit*)

PRACTICE: To help the students practice, I told them that they were going to need to listen very carefully because we were going to tell a story about our words when we were finished. I asked,

"What is *ran* without the /r/?" (*an*)

"What if we add /c/ to the beginning? (*can*)

"What if we add /p/ to the beginning? (*pan*)

"What if we add /m/ to the beginning? (*man*)

Next, the students repeated the words after me and we thought about a sentence we could say that used the words. We decided to start with "The man," and we knew we needed to use *can* and *pan*. So, we said, "The man can use the pan to cook." When we had said our sentence, we talked about what it meant. The students said that a pan was like a pot and the man could use the pan to cook dinner. Then the students drew what the sentence meant.

REFLECT: The students seemed to understand our work with deleting and adding phonemes. They all commented on how fun it was to change the sounds to make different words.

Student-Facilitated Center and Routine

LISTENING CENTER: My students have their own tapes that they brought in from home at the start of the school year. On various occasions, the students tape themselves singing, reading, or answering questions. Then I can go back and check their work on the tape. At this center, the students listened to their tapes, on which I (with the help of our cross-age buddies) had prerecorded several sets of words, phoneme deletions, and phoneme additions. The students then recorded their responses with the help of their cross-age partners.

CROSS-AGE READING EXPERIENCES: My students worked with their third-grade reading buddies to play phoneme baseball. Before playing the game, I went to visit the third graders and explained what they would be doing and how to help their partners if they needed assistance. The students were given a picture of a baseball diamond that contained home plate, first base, second base, and third base. Each of my students was given a game piece to move around the bases. The third graders gave my students a beginning word. To move to first base, they had to change the beginning sound to make a new word. To move to second base, they had to take a new word and change the middle sound to make a new word. To move to third base, they had to take a new word and change the ending sound to make a new word. At home plate, the student had to say the final word they had created. The third graders kept track of how many runs their students scored. If the younger students needed help, their third-grade buddies were able to assist them. The list of words that was given to the third graders included *pet, big, rug, sun, sit, tug, rip, run,* and *bat*. The Cross-Age Reading Experiences concluded with two sets of buddies reading books that promote phonemic awareness, such as *Sheep in a Jeep* (Shaw) and *Does a Kangaroo Have a Mother Too?* (Carle) (see Appendix A, p.177).

STAGE 3   Teacher-Facilitated Whole-Group Reflection

SHARE: The students shared their cross-age reading experiences with the class. The children enjoyed talking about their time with their buddies.

REFLECT: Once again we discussed the importance of being able to change sounds to make new words. We talked about how being able to do this would later help us to read and write many new words.

SET NEW GOALS: The students enjoyed using phoneme deletion and addition, although they needed continued reinforcement. We decided to stay with our current goal and spend more time learning and practicing phoneme deletion and addition.

Assessment Options

I observed students through most stages of the lesson and listened to each student's tape-recorded responses. Students also engaged in peer assessment with their buddies during phoneme baseball. If students had difficulty, their buddies helped them but they talked to me about them later in our quick conferences, which took only about a minute with each student.

Final Thoughts on This Chapter

The lessons in this chapter integrated research findings and current beliefs about best practice in teaching phonemic awareness. The research-based Guided Comprehension Model for the Primary Grades provided a format that integrated direct and guided instruction as well as numerous opportunities for independent practice. Texts at a variety of levels and various modes of reader response were incorporated to accommodate students' abilities. Reflection and informal assessments permeated the lessons, which were designed to foster students' understanding of phonemic awareness.

It's important to note that although the lessons featured in this chapter were taught at particular grade levels, they can be adapted to accommodate other levels and needs. For example, all of these lessons were taught in kindergarten, but if first-, second- or third-grade students (or even upper-grade students) have not mastered phonemic awareness, the lessons can be used to teach them its different aspects. Students develop at their own rates and their needs for different skills and strategies vary.

Ideas to adapt the lessons to accommodate English-Language Learners, struggling readers, and special needs students include changing the level of the texts (see Appendix A, p. 177, for a list of alternative texts), adding more modeling and demonstration, providing more examples or focusing on fewer examples, providing time for more guided instruction or independent practice, and changing the level of word choice or questioning. These lessons address skills that develop over time and continue to need reinforcement.

In the next chapter, we examine the role of phonics in the reading process. We begin by addressing its theoretical underpinnings and then present a variety of lessons focused on teaching phonics in the primary grades.

What can we read to learn more about teaching phonemic awareness?

Yopp, H. K. (1992). Developing phonemic awareness in young children. *The Reading Teacher, 45*, 696–703.

Yopp, H. K. (1995). Read-aloud books for developing phonemic awareness: An annotated bibliography. *The Reading Teacher, 48*, 538–542.

Yopp, H. K., & Yopp, R. H. (2000). Supporting phonemic awareness development in the classroom. *The Reading Teacher, 54*, 130–143.

CHAPTER 3

Phonics

Phonics has been the source of some controversy in past decades, but it is now considered to be one of the five building blocks of literacy. Many of us can recall learning from little plaid phonics books, but today's students experience phonics in a different context—embedded within balanced reading programs as a natural part of literacy instruction.

In this chapter, we focus on teaching phonics in the primary grades. In Part One, we explain what phonics is, present what the research has to say, and discuss how to integrate the research results in our teaching. In Part Two, we present teacher-authored, classroom-tested, strategy-based Guided Comprehension lessons focused on different ideas for teaching phonics. The chapter concludes with final thoughts and a short list of suggested readings.

Part One: Research Base

What is phonics?

"Phonics is a way of teaching reading and spelling that stresses symbol-sound relationships, used especially in beginning instruction" (Harris & Hodges, 1995, p. 186).

What does the research tell us?

The reading process is generally acknowledged to have three cueing systems: graphophonic, syntactic, and semantic. In the graphophonic cueing system, the phoneme or sound is combined with the grapheme or written letter. The syntactic cueing system involves language order, sentence structure, and parts of speech. The semantic cueing system focuses on making sense. All three cueing systems interact simultaneously.

Research reports that systematic phonics instruction benefits students in the elementary grades, including students who have difficulty learning to read. Benefits to students in the primary grades have included increased ability to read and spell words in kindergarten and to decode, spell, and comprehend in first grade. Students in the upper elementary grades who received systematic phonics instruction were also better able to decode and spell, but their comprehension did not show significant improvement.

Other outcomes of research in phonics include the following:

- It should be taught along with phonemic awareness, phonics, fluency, vocabulary, and comprehension, as part of a balanced reading program.

- It can and should be taught in entertaining and creative ways.

- Teachers should assess students' individual needs and tailor instruction to meet those needs (National Reading Panel, 2000).

How can we make the research-teaching connection?

The research supports that phonics is an integral component of literacy instruction and should be taught as part of a balanced literacy program. In Part Two of this chapter, we present a variety of Guided Comprehension lessons designed to facilitate this process. The lessons feature direct and guided instruction, as well as opportunities for independent practice in centers and routines. Additional ideas for teaching phonics can be found in Appendix C (p. 182).

Part Two: Lesson Overview

In this chapter, all of the lessons focus on phonics. Featured texts include *An ABC Bestiary* (Blackwell, 1989), *Matthew A.B.C.* (Catalanotto, 2002), *Eating the Alphabet: Fruits and Vegetables* (Ehlert, 1982), *Mrs. Wishy-Washy's Farm* (Cowley, 2003), *Froggy Goes to School* (London, 1996), *Bear Wants More* (Wilson, 2003), *Aunt Lucy Went to Buy a Hat* (Low, 2004), and *Sheep in a Jeep* (Shaw, 1986). Appendix A (p. 177) contains a list of additional texts that can be used for phonics instruction.

The lessons in this chapter are appropriate for all different types of learners. In our classrooms we may have students who speak English as a second language, struggling readers, and students with special needs. To accommodate these learners, the lessons include the use of multiple modalities (singing, sketching, and so on) working with partners, books on tape, cross-age experiences, and extra guided instruction for students who struggle. For ideas on further adapting the lessons, see "Final Thoughts" at the end of the chapter.

This section features six teacher-authored, classroom-tested lessons that each address a specific aspect of or idea for teaching phonics including working with letters and sounds, Making Words, Making and Writing Words, using Onset and Rime Word Walls, and working with word families. The lessons are teacher-authored and feature student work. They were designed using the Guided Comprehension Model for the Primary Grades (McLaughlin, 2003), which was discussed in Chapter 1.

LESSON 1 Alphabet Letters and Sounds

STAGE 1 Teacher-Directed Whole-Group Instruction

TEXT: *An ABC Bestiary* (Blackwell, 1989)

EXPLAIN: I explained to students that we would be working with our letters and sounds as we learned some verbs or action words. I asked students to stand while I explained what we would be doing today. I said, "We are going to use this book to learn more about action words or verbs. *Run*, *jump*, and *dance* are some examples of action words or verbs. We call them action words because they require us to do something. What action do you think *run* requires us to do?" The students started running in place. I said, "That's right. The action is running. Now, show me what the action is for *jump*." The students started jumping. I said, "That's right. The action is jumping. Will you show me the action for *dancing*?" All of the students danced near their desks. I thanked them for their help, then explained that we would be learning new action words and using our letters and sounds to read them. I told the students that the book I would be reading was *An ABC Bestiary*, an alphabet book about animals. I introduced the book and opened it to display the first page. It said, "Aardvark arranging art." I said, "In this book, every page has a letter of the alphabet." (I pointed to and said "Aa.") "There are also words that start with that letter." (I pointed to "Aardvark arranging art.") "One of the words is always an animal name." (I pointed to *aardvark* and before I could say it, Tommy said, "Aardvark. He's an aardvark. That's what Arthur is." He was, of course, referring to Arthur the aardvark, the main character in Marc Brown's books.) Next, I said, "One of the words is always an action word or verb." (I pointed to *arranging* and said it.) Then I asked what the action was in the action word *arranging*, and the students started arranging things on the tops of their desks. Finally, I said "I will read the book aloud and we will identify the action words, and discuss them as we read." I reminded the students to listen carefully to the beginning sounds and letters of each word.

DEMONSTRATE: Before reading the book aloud, I reviewed the letter-sound correspondences that we had been working on. I used my letter cards that each have a letter of the alphabet written on the front. I asked the students to say the letter name and sound. Then various students volunteered a word that began with each sound. For example, Jackie said, "M says /m/, and a word that starts with /m/ is *mouse*." Next, I wrote the letters *f, c*, and *r* on the board. I reminded the students that in the book *An ABC Bestiary*, there were names of animals that began with each letter of the alphabet. Then I demonstrated using one of the letters I had written on the board. I said, "*Frog* begins with the letter *f*, which has the sound /f/. Then the students offered examples for *c* and *r*. Alejandro used *cat* for *c*, and Lindsay used *rabbit* for *r*.

GUIDE: I reminded the students to listen carefully for animal names and action words as I read the book aloud. I explained that we would discuss each animal and action word and then someone could volunteer to act out the meaning of the verb. I paused at various points to discuss the animal names and action words that started with that letter of the alphabet. For example, the Ee page said, "Elephant exploring Ecuador." We noted that *elephant* was an animal that started with *e*. Next, the students pointed out that *exploring* was the action word and a few of the students explained what it meant to explore. David acted out what he thought exploring looked like. The Ff page said, "Frog fixing flat." I asked the students which word was the animal's name and which word was the action word. Ben said, "*Frog* is the animal's name and *fixing* is the action word." Then he acted out fixing a tire. We continued doing this with selected pages throughout the book. The students especially enjoyed acting out the verbs. When I finished reading, I explained to the students that we were going to think of a different action word for each letter of the alphabet. I showed them a transparency of the ABCs on the overhead. We went through each letter of the alphabet and said an action word that began with that letter. I wrote the action words on the transparency and then we all acted out what we thought the words meant. Here are the action words the students suggested for each letter:

Aa act	**Bb** bounce	**Cc** catch	**Dd** dance
Ee enter	**Ff** fall	**Gg** gallop	**Hh** hop
Ii itch	**Jj** jump	**Kk** kick	**Ll** lick
Mm march	**Nn** nod	**Oo** open	**Pp** pick
Qq quit	**Rr** run	**Ss** sit	**Tt** talk
Uu unlace	**Vv** vacuum	**Ww** watch	**Xx** eXit
Yy yawn	**Zz** zip		

As often happens in alphabet activities, we could not think of an action word that begins with *Xx*, so we used *exit*, a word that begins with the sound /x/, and wrote it in a way that emphasizes the *x*: eXit.

PRACTICE: To practice, I organized the students in small groups. I gave each group an ABC paper like the one I had used to write the ABC action words. Then they worked together to think of different animal names for each letter of the alphabet. If the students needed help thinking of animals, they were able to use a variety of animal books that I had provided at each table. When students had finished, we shared the different animal names they had written in alphabetical order. As students shared an animal name, they also said a sentence about the animal. For example, Dana and Kim said, "L is for *llama*," and provided the sentence "Llamas have mamas," which was based on a book we had recently read. After we discussed each animal, we reviewed the spellings, and students sketched an animal and wrote a sentence about it. Makeda's drawing and sentence are featured in Figure 3-1.

REFLECT: The students reflected on the importance of knowing their letters and beginning sounds to help them think of different action words and animals for each letter of the alphabet. The students said they liked thinking of different animal names and action words with their peers and they enjoyed acting out the action words.

FIGURE 3-1

(STAGE 2) Teacher-Guided Small-Group Instruction

TEXT: *Matthew A.B.C.* (Catalanotto, 2002)

REVIEW: To review, we discussed the importance of knowing our letters and sounds. I told the students that a lot of the activities we would be working on this week would deal with knowing our letters and sounds, so we quickly reviewed them. I explained to the students that I was going to read them another ABC book, called *Matthew A.B.C.* I also told the students that after I read the book to them they were going to be writing their own ABC books.

GUIDE: I read the story *Matthew A.B.C.* to the students. In this book, the teacher has 26 students in her class, all named Matthew. The principal wonders how the teacher tells them all apart. Each Matthew happens to have a last name that begins with a different letter of the alphabet, so the teacher distinguishes each Matthew by associating his last name with a different word or object that starts with the same letter. As I was reading, I stopped and had the students try to predict what word or object the teacher might say for the next letter. For example, before we got to Matthew K., I had the children predict what the teacher might say for him. Kendra said, "The teacher might say Matthew K. has a kitten." The book said, "Matthew K. is unusually fond of ketchup."

PRACTICE: To practice, I had the students write their own *Matthew A.B.C.* books, but instead of using Matthew, they used their first names. For example, Emily's book was entitled *Emily A.B.C.* and Josh's was *Josh A.B.C.* I provided the students with blank books, which I had created by stapling sheets of paper together. The students patterned their books after the one I had read, so each of the pages in their books also represented a different letter of the alphabet. As the students wrote their books, I helped them with their writing and spelling if they needed assistance. Then the students illustrated their books at the art center. Writing and illustrating the alphabet books took a few days to finish, but when they were complete, the students shared them and we created a special section of our classroom library to display them. Figure 3-2 contains a sample page from Pablo's ABC book.

FIGURE 3-2

REFLECT: We discussed how knowing our letters and sounds helps us read and that learning them can be fun. The students noted that they enjoyed creating their own ABC books. They shared their books with the class when they were finished. Students gave their classmates feedback and compliments about the books they had created.

Student-Facilitated Centers

ABC CENTER: Students went on an alphabet scavenger hunt. Each student took a paper with particular letters of the alphabet on it. Then they walked around the classroom and found objects that started with each of the letters on their sheet. They wrote the names of the objects next to the appropriate letters. I provided the students with clipboards to use to make it easier for them to write.

ART CENTER: Students illustrated the ABC books they created during small-group instruction.

MAKE-A-BOOK CENTER: Students created alphabet scrapbooks. I prepared a blank book for each student by stapling together sheets of paper. The students wrote a different letter of the alphabet in order on each page. Then they either cut out pictures in magazines of objects that began with the letter on each page or they drew pictures of objects. The next week at the ABC center, the students finished their alphabet scrapbooks and began labeling their pictures. Figure 3-3 shows sample pages from Darren's alphabet scrapbook. (Later in the year, the students added sight words to their scrapbooks, so they became more like personal dictionaries.)

FIGURE 3-3

(STAGE 3) Teacher-Facilitated Whole-Group Reflection

SHARE: We began by discussing the scavenger hunt and sharing some of the items the students had found. Everyone listened carefully to the letter sound and the beginning sound of each of the object names. Then the students shared the ABC books they began creating in small groups and the alphabet scrapbooks they had completed at the Make-a-Book Center.

REFLECT: Students reflected on the importance of knowing their letters and sounds to help them read, spell, and write. We also discussed the importance of reading ABC books to help us identify sounds and words that start with the different letters of the alphabet.

SET NEW GOALS: We decided to continue our work with letters and sounds. We also decided to continue working with the alphabet by reading and writing other alphabet books.

Assessment Options

Observation was the assessment that I used most often during this lesson. I also reviewed and commented on the books the students made and listened carefully when they provided feedback about their peers' books.

LESSON 2 Making Words

STAGE 1 Teacher-Directed Whole-Group Instruction

TEXT: *Eating the Alphabet: Fruits and Vegetables from A to Z* (Ehlert, 1982)

EXPLAIN: As part of a theme on food and nutrition, we worked on making various food words. I explained to the students that we would be Making Words (adapted from Cunningham, 2000). We were going to try to form words out of different letters. The letters that we were going to use to form the words were from food or nutrition words that we had been learning about in our theme.

DEMONSTRATE: To demonstrate, I brought out my magnetic letters and moved the letters *a, t, s, h,* and *c* to the whiteboard. I told the students that we would be making words from these five letters. I used the letters to form the word *cat*. I asked the students if they saw another word we could form using those letters. Cheryl said, "We can make *at*." Ava saw the word *hat*. I asked her to come up and move the letters to form *hat*. Alexander said, "We can make the word *sat*," and he came and moved the letters to form *sat*. I asked, "Do you notice a pattern in the words we just made?" They discovered that all of the words fit into the *-at* family. Next, I explained that we were going to work together to form two-letter, three-letter, four-letter, and five-letter words using our magnetic letters. I said, "We will keep making words until we use all of the letters we are working with to form a mystery word." Then I gave a clue. I said, "This time the mystery word will be a food word that we will be reading about."

GUIDE: Before we started the Making Words activity, I introduced and read aloud *Eating the Alphabet: Fruits and Vegetables from A–Z,* by Lois Ehlert. I told students that the letters we would be using were from a word found in the book. I also gave them another clue. I said, "Our mystery word is a fruit." I placed the letters *r, g, a, e, n, s,* and *o* on the board. (I used magnetic letters on the whiteboard. Magnetic letters also work well on cookie sheets.) I asked the students if they saw any two-letter words using these letters. Susanne saw the word *as* and came to the board to move the magnetic letters to form the word. Justin formed the word *or*. Then students took turns at their desks forming new words out of the letters. They found three-letter words next. They were able to form the following words with some direction from me: *gas, sag, nag, rag,* and *age.* If the students were not seeing a word, I prompted them by saying, "Can you form another word by changing one letter in the word?" Next, we tried forming some four-letter words. I told them the first word we would form was *sage.* One student came up and formed the word for us. Then I asked another student to change the first letter in *sage* to form the word *rage.* Next, I helped the students form some five-letter words. I told them I saw the word *anger,* and Louis helped me form the word. I told the students there were many more words we could form but that it was time to guess the mystery word. I reminded them that we would need to use all of the letters and the mystery word was a fruit. Several students figured out the word and helped to form *oranges.*

PRACTICE: To practice, I gave each student an envelope with the letters *r, a, c, f,* and *j* inside. Then I said, "These letters do not make a mystery word. They are just to use as we practice moving our magnetic letters on our individual whiteboards." Next, I asked the students if they could form a two-letter word. They said they couldn't, but Allison noticed the word family *-ar.* I asked if they could form the word *car* and they did. Next I asked the students to change one letter in *car* to form *far* and they did. Finally, they changed one letter in *far* to form *jar.* The students were very pleased with their work. They moved their letters with ease and formed all of the words. I told them that we would be working with letters to form new words later in the day.

REFLECT: We reflected that we could form many new words using just a small number of letters. We talked about finding patterns in the letters to help us form words. James said, "Once I figured out the pattern (*-ar*), I was able to see lots of words."

(STAGE 2) Teacher-Guided Small-Group Instruction

REVIEW: To review, I explained that we would be forming new words using a variety of letters and that the last word we would make would be a mystery word. I reminded students to look for patterns to help them form new words. I also gave them a clue: I said, "The mystery word is another fruit we have read about."

GUIDE: To guide students, I used my magnetic letters on the whiteboard and formed the words as they did. The students each had a set of magnetic letters and an individual whiteboard that they could use to form the words. I also prompted the students by providing clues to words that were more difficult to find.

PRACTICE: To practice, I gave each student the following letter cards: *p, l, a, e, s*, and another *p*. I asked the students to form a two-letter word using *s* and *a*. They formed *as*. I asked them to form a two-letter word that is a man's name. They formed *Al*. Then I asked the students whether they could form a three-letter word by placing *p* in front of *Al*. They formed *pal*. I asked the students to form the word *lap*. Then they changed the first letter to form *sap*. Next, I asked the students to take away the *s* and add an *e* to try to form a new word. The word they formed was *ape*. I asked them to rearrange those letters to form the word *pea*. Next, I asked them to change the *p* to an *s* to form a new word. The students said the word was *sea*. Then we moved on to four-letter words, and the students formed *slap*. I asked them to rearrange the letters in *slap* to form *pals*. One student noticed that he could make the word *apes*. He remembered that we had made *ape* earlier and noticed we had an *s*. I asked the students to rearrange the letters in *apes* to form *peas*. Then I asked if they had figured out the mystery word yet. I reminded the students that they would need to use all of the letters to spell the mystery word. Gracie guessed that the mystery word was *apples*, and we all formed the word.

REFLECT: The students explained that they thought making words was easier when they got to move the letters. I was happy to learn that they felt comfortable manipulating the letters. Kayla said, "I liked when you gave us clues to help us figure out the words," and Adam said, "We can make lots of words!"

Student-Facilitated Center

MAKING WORDS CENTER: Students worked with partners to make words out of the following letters: *e, d, n, p, s*, and *s*. The students each had magnetic letters on a cookie sheet, which they could manipulate to make new words. The partners helped each other figure out new words and patterns. I reminded them to start with two-letter words first and then to move to three-, four-, and five-letter words, if they could. Students did not have to write the words; I just wanted them to get practice manipulating the letters. Some of the words they formed were *Ed, Ned, end, den, pen, pens, dens, send, sped, spend*, and *spends*.

STAGE 3   Teacher-Facilitated Whole-Group Reflection

SHARE: Students shared some of the words they had made in Stage 2. We talked about the words and had fun using them in our conversation. Jeffrey made up this silly sentence with his center words: "Ned spends all his money on pens."

REFLECT: Students reflected on how they could form many words from the same letters. They explained that it was harder to do on their own with a partner than it was to do with me. I reminded them that this was the first time they had done this activity and that they would have much more practice. The students said they enjoyed making words, and their favorite part was figuring out the mystery word.

Assessment Options

I used a lot of observation during this lesson and recorded notes about students' performance. I was especially focused on students' abilities to manipulate their letters and form different words. The information I recorded helped me to identify students who were having difficulties.

LESSON 3   Making and Writing Words

STAGE 1   Teacher-Directed Whole-Group Instruction

EXPLAIN: As part of our unit on animals, I explained that we would be Making and Writing Words (Rasinski, 1999a) from different animal names. We had been manipulating letter cards and magnetic letters to form new words for some time now, but this would be the first time students would be writing the words. I said to the students, "We usually move our magnetic letters to make words on our whiteboards. Today we are going to use our journals to write the words we create." I reminded students to look for patterns with the letters to help them form words. I also reminded them to start with two-letter words, then move on to three-letter, four-letter, and so on.

DEMONSTRATE: To demonstrate what we would be doing, I used a transparency and the overhead projector. I wrote the letters *c*, *p*, *a*, *t*, *s*, and *l* at the top of the transparency and asked the students to write the same letters in their journals. Then we started forming two-letter words. I wrote the words *at* and *Al*. Then I showed them we could form three-letter words such as *pat, cat, sat, cap, tap*. I wrote those words on the transparency and asked the students to write them in their journals. Next, I showed them how we could form the four-letter words *cats, laps,* and *slap*. I wrote the words on the overhead and the students wrote them in their journals. We talked about the words, noticed some patterns we knew, and used them in fun sentences. Jenny said the sentence, "The cats swam laps in the pond."

GUIDE: To guide students, I gave them the letters in the word *animals* to use when Making and Writing Words. I wrote the letters randomly on the overhead and then I encouraged the students to copy them. I asked them to make and write two-letter words. They wrote *an* and *am*. For three-letter words, they wrote *Sam* and *aim*. Then they wrote these four-, five-, and six-letter words: *main, mail, nail, sail, slam, slim; snail, nasal; salami, animal*. Then I reminded the students that the mystery word would contain all of the letters we had been using. They guessed *animals* and they wrote it in their journals. I gave the students some clues to help them form some of the words, especially when it came to the larger words, but many of the students picked up on the *-ail* word family to form the words *mail, nail,* and *snail*.

PRACTICE: To practice, students worked with partners to make and write new words out of the letters in the word *turtles*, which I gave to them in random order. The words that many of the students wrote were *let, set, rut, use, rust, rest, test, true, user, rule, rules, trust,* and *turtles*. After the students had worked with their partners to form many words, we talked about what we knew about the words and how we could use them in our reading, writing, and conversations.

REFLECT: We reflected on how it was easier to write the words because we had done so much practicing by using letter cards and magnetic letters. Some of the students explained that it was more fun to form the words without me because it was like a puzzle to figure out the words on their own.

(STAGE 2) Teacher-Guided Small-Group Instruction

REVIEW: We reviewed by discussing Making and Writing Words and how it helped us learn more words. Then I reminded the students that they would be writing in their journals the words they made.

GUIDE: To guide the students, I gave them the letters in the word *tigers* in random order. Each student copied the letters, and I prompted them to think of words. First, I asked the students if they saw any two-letter words. They all wrote *is* and *it*. Then I suggested that they make three-letter words using those patterns. They could only form the word *sit*. Next, I asked the students if they saw a pattern we could use. One student noticed the pattern *-et*, so they wrote *set* and *get*. For four-letter words, they wrote *stir*, *tire*, *rise*, and *rest*. I helped them with the five-letter words *tires* and *tries*, but they guessed the mystery word and they wrote *tigers*.

PRACTICE: To practice, I had the students work by themselves to see how many words they could make from the letters in *kittens*, which I gave them in random order. After some time working on their own, we discussed the words that they had written. I observed that a few students were having difficulty because they had only come up with a few words. I kept working with those students in small groups until they were successful at Making and Writing Words.

REFLECT: Most of the students were finding success in Making and Writing Words. Rashawn said, "I feel like I still need to use the magnetic letters to form words." I responded by telling him and the rest of the students that they could still use the magnetic letters if they wanted to. They could move the magnetic letters and then write in their journals the words they had formed. A few of the students who were feeling that Making and Writing Words was challenging were happy to hear this. Then we reflected on how everything we learned built on what we already knew.

Student-Facilitated Center and Routine

MAKING WORDS CENTER: Students chose an animal name (letters in random order) from a list I had provided and wrote it in their journals. Then they used the letters for Making and Writing Words. The animal names on the list were *chickens, elephants, goldfish, lizards, panthers, parrots, rabbits, reindeer, roosters,* and *spiders.*

CROSS-AGE READING EXPERIENCES: The students worked with their third-grade reading buddies to make and write words using the letters in *starfish*. Some of the words they wrote were *at*, *sat*, *hat*, *rat*, *tar*, *far*, *air*, *hair*, *fair*, *fish*, *star*, *stir*, *stair*, *stars*, *stairs*, and *starfish*.

(STAGE 3) Teacher-Facilitated Whole-Group Reflection

SHARE: The students shared the work they did with their cross-age buddies and talked about how much they enjoyed making words with them.

REFLECT: We reflected on how we looked for different patterns to help us create new words. We also talked about how we used our eyes to see the patterns instead of moving letter cards to see the patterns, and that seemed to be a sign of progress to the students.

SET NEW GOALS: We decided that we needed more practice in Making and Writing Words, so we planned to practice doing it when we visited the center and at home.

Assessment Options

I observed students making and writing words on their own, with peers, and with their cross-age partners. I took notes throughout the various stages of the lesson and continued to work with the students who were still having difficulty.

LESSON 4 Guess the Covered Word

(STAGE 1) Teacher-Directed Whole-Group Instruction

TEXT: *Mrs. Wishy-Washy's Farm* (Cowley, 2003)

EXPLAIN: I explained to students that sometimes when we read, we come to words that we may not know. I told them that when this happens we can use clues to help us figure out the word. I said, "To practice this, we will be trying to Guess the Covered Word. To figure out the words, we will use clues from other words" (Cunningham, 2000). I explained that I would also provide clues by revealing the letters in the word, one by one.

DEMONSTRATE: To demonstrate to the students, I had written a few sentences on the board. I had covered up one word in each sentence, and I explained that we would need to figure them out. The first sentence read: "The boy hit the ball with a _____." I asked the students to first guess what word they thought went into each blank. I showed them the first letter in the missing word. I revealed a *b* as the first letter. The students told me they thought the word was *bat*. The sentence would read: "The boy hit the ball with a bat." The students were correct. I revealed the rest of the letters and showed them the whole sentence. If the students had been incorrect, I would have revealed the next letter in the word, and continued doing this until they figured out the word. I also used the sentence: "We had _____ for lunch on Friday." I revealed the first letter. It was *p*. The students guessed *pizza* right away, but I showed them how I would have revealed each letter.

GUIDE: To guide the students, I introduced and read aloud the big book *Mrs. Wishy-Washy's Farm*. Before reading the book aloud, I had gone through the book and covered up various words with colored removable tape. As I read the story aloud, I had the students guess what the covered words were. First, students guessed at the words by using the context clues and picture clues. Then I uncovered the letters one at a time, until the students figured out the word. For example, one sentence read: "This is Mrs. Wishy-Washy and this is her _____." The missing word was *farm*. Many students first guessed *house*, but when I revealed the first letter was *f*, they guessed it was *farm*. Then I revealed all of the letters, so they would know they were correct. I continued reading the entire book and having children guess all of the covered words.

PRACTICE: To practice, I gave the students copies of several sentences that had words missing. First, they went through and wrote what words they thought fit, using the context clues. When they finished, we discussed their predictions and I revealed the first letter of each missing word. I showed them the first letter by putting the sentences on the overhead. By this time, most students had figured out the missing words, but I was careful to show them a transparency in which all of the letters had been revealed. Here are examples of some of the sentences:

The teacher was _____ a song on the piano. (*playing*)

At school, I like to sit by my _____. (*friend*)

The school bell _____ when it was time to go home. (*rang*)

SHARE: We shared ideas about knowing how words work. We focused on Making Words, Making and Writing Words, and Guess the Covered Word.

REFLECT: We reflected on the importance of using picture and context clues when reading. We also discussed the importance of checking the sounds of words to see if they matched the word we read. We might think the word makes sense, but we always have to double-check the sounds to make sure we are reading the correct word.

STAGE 2   Teacher-Guided Small-Group Instruction

TEXT: *Froggy Goes to School* (London, 1996)

REVIEW: To review, I reminded students to look for picture clues and context clues when they come to words they don't know. I reminded them to look at the sounds to determine whether the word they guessed matches the letter sounds.

GUIDE: To guide the students, I read aloud to them the story *Froggy Goes to School*. Before reading the story, I had gone through and covered various words with the colored removable tape. As I read the story, I stopped and had the students guess what the covered word was. They first guessed a word they thought made sense and then I gave them the letter clues.

PRACTICE: To practice guessing the covered words, the students wrote four sentences in their best handwriting. I helped each student use the colored removable tape to cover up one word in each sentence. Then I assigned partners, and they guessed each other's covered words. After the words were correctly guessed, the tape was fully removed to reveal the covered word. An example of one of Matt's sentences was "The frog jumped in the _____." (*lake*)

REFLECT: We reflected on the importance of double-checking the sounds against the words that we thought fit the blank. Alicia said she was sure the word *pond* fit into the last sentence, but the first letter that was revealed was an *l*. That caused her to revise her predictions and guess another word.

Student-Facilitated Center and Routine

WRITING CENTER: Students wrote four more sentences and used the colored tape to cover a word. They worked with their partners and guessed each other's covered words. They were sure to reveal all of the letters after the words were guessed.

CROSS-AGE READING EXPERIENCES: My students were read books by their third-grade reading buddies. With guidance from their teacher, the third graders chose the books to read to their partners. They had already covered several words before they came to our class. My students guessed the covered words, as we had done previously in class.

(STAGE 3) Teacher-Facilitated Whole-Group Reflection

SHARE: Students shared their sentences from center time and asked us to guess their covered words.

REFLECT: We reflected again on the importance of using all of our clues when trying to figure out unknown words. I reminded the students that it was important to look not only at the beginning sounds in the word, but also at the ending sounds.

SET NEW GOALS: We decided to extend our learning about context clues and Guess the Covered Word to informational text.

Assessment Options

I observed students for several purposes, including guessing the covered word, using context clues, and contributing to discussion.

LESSON 5 Onset/Rime Word Wall

STAGE 1 Teacher-Directed Whole-Group Instruction

TEXT: *Bear Wants More* (Wilson, 2003)

EXPLAIN: I explained to the students that we would be reading the book *Bear Wants More* by Karma Wilson. I told them that after reading the story we would be working with onsets and rimes. I explained that rimes were the part of the word from the first vowel onward; in *game*, *-ame* is the rime. The letter or letters before the first vowels are the onset. So, in the word *game*, *g* would be the onset. I explained that we would be working with the rime *-ore*, as in the word *more* from our story. I reminded the students that the *m* in *more* would be the onset. We were going to see how many different words we could make by placing different onsets in front of *-ore*. We had learned about onset and rime when we created our Onset and Rime Word Wall (see Appendix D, p. 184). I reminded students that we can form many words by adding different onsets to the same rime. (On our Onset and Rime Word Wall, the onsets were in black print and the rimes were in red. They were attached to the wall with Velcro to make it easy to add, remove, or make new words.)

DEMONSTRATE: Before introducing and reading the story, I demonstrated again that we could form many words from the various rimes by just putting new letters, or onsets, in front of the rime. I used the example *-at*. I had the students come up and help me write words using *-at*. They came up with *cat*, *bat*, *hat*, *sat*, *rat*, *fat*, *mat*, *pat*, *that*, *splat*, *chat*, *drat*, and *flat*.

GUIDE: I introduced *Bear Wants More* and read it to the students. When we finished the story, I took the rime *-ore* from our Onset and Rime Word Wall and showed that by adding *m*, I would create *more*, which we had just read in the story. Next, I asked the students to help me brainstorm another onset we could use to make a word. Samantha said, "We can make the word *core*, like the core of an apple." Some of the other words we came up with were *bore*, *tore*, *wore*, *fore*, *shore*, *snore*, *sore*, and *store*. Then we spent some time discussing the words, using them in sentences, and acting out words such as *bore* and *snore*.

PRACTICE: To practice, the students created their own bears from various craft materials I gave them. They received a small brown lunch bag, brown paper, and markers. They made a bear's head, arms, and legs on their brown paper. They used their markers to decorate and add details. They then glued the body parts to the brown paper bag. The paper bag was used as the body. Next, the students each used ten index cards, writing an *-ore* word on each card. (We had created the words earlier together on our Onset and Rime Word Wall, but we did not write them down.) In the story we had read earlier, Bear always wanted more to eat, so we fed our bears more *-ore* words. We put the *-ore* words into the bag as if it were the bear's belly. The students took their bears home to share the story of *Bear Wants More* with their families. They also practiced reading their *-ore* words to an adult or older sibling.

REFLECT: We reflected on the observation that we can use our Onset and Rime Word Wall to help us form many new words. We discussed that being able to form these new words helps us with our reading and writing of new words.

STAGE 2 — Teacher-Guided Small-Group Instruction

REVIEW: We reviewed how to form new words by using our Onset and Rime Word Wall and discussed how we could connect onset and rimes to books as we did with *Bear Wants More.*

GUIDE: To guide the students, I pulled the rime *-ot* off the word wall. (See Appendix D, p.184, for information about word walls.) The group immediately started adding onsets to create words. Our list included *cot, rot, dot, tot, got, hot, blot, knot, lot, plot, not, trot, pot, shot,* and *spot.* Emma said, "It's easy now to make new words with the Onset and Rime Word Wall. I just keep trying new onsets with the rime until a word makes sense."

PRACTICE: To practice, the students chose any rime they wanted from the word wall. Iris pulled down the rime *-op* and used it to form the words *bop, crop, cop, drop, hop, prop, mop, shop, pop, stop, top, flop,* and *chop.* After the students had written all of the words they could by adding onsets to their rime, I explained to the students that we could use our brainstormed lists to create what was called a "hink pink." I explained that to create a hink pink we would need to choose two rhyming words that created a funny object or thought. Then we could turn them into riddles. I gave the example of *fat cat.* I said, "My riddle is, what do you call a cat that ate too much?" They all laughed and said, "A fat cat." Iris, who created *-op* words, came up with *pop shop.* Her riddle was, "Where do you get a cold drink on a hot day?" At a pop shop. Some hink pinks that other students thought of using their words were *pink drink, cold gold, brain strain, long song, broom room,* and *low blow.* The students drew pictures and wrote riddles to go along with their hink pinks.

REFLECT: Students shared how fun it was to create hink pinks. They wanted to create more of them. I told them they could do that at center time. The students also shared that it was fun creating different words using the Onset and Rime Word Wall.

Student-Facilitated Centers

MAKING WORDS CENTER: Students worked with partners to create more hink pinks using the Onset and Rime Word Wall. Then they illustrated them and wrote their hink-pink riddles.

WRITING CENTER: Students wrote letters to classmates using as many onset and rime words as possible. The classmates who received the letters then responded in the same way. Students delivered and picked up their mail at our class mailbox, where each student had a mail slot with his or her name on it.

(STAGE 3) Teacher-Facilitated Whole-Group Reflection

SHARE: Students shared their hink-pink riddles and illustrations with the class. The students all tried to guess what the answers were.

REFLECT: We discussed how we can use our Onset and Rime Word Wall to help us form many new words. We talked about how important the different rimes were in helping us with our reading, writing, and spelling.

SET NEW GOALS: The students were beginning to feel comfortable using onsets and rimes, so we decided to make our own onset and rime word wheels and flip charts.

Assessment Options

I used observation throughout the lesson. I also recorded notes on students as they worked in small groups and provided extra support for students who seemed to be having difficulty creating words using onsets and rimes.

LESSON 6 Word Families

STAGE 1 Teacher-Directed Whole-Group Instruction

TEXT: *Aunt Lucy Went to Buy a Hat* (Low, 2004)

EXPLAIN: I explained to students that we would be working with the word family *-at*. We had previously discussed what a word family was. Kelsey shared with the group that a word family is a group of words that all have the same group of sounds in them, but different beginnings. Anthony said, "Word families are like rimes. We can make lots of words with them."

DEMONSTRATE: To demonstrate, I used the word family *-ap*. I drew a house on a piece of poster paper. I then wrote *-ap* on the roof of the house. I demonstrated what a word family was by writing various *-ap* words inside the house. The words I wrote were *cap, gap, tap, zap, lap, clap, trap, map, nap, flap, rap, slap, sap,* and *snap*. I told the students that all of these words are in the *-ap* family. They all live together in their "word family house."

GUIDE: To guide the students, I introduced and read aloud the story *Aunt Lucy Went to Buy a Hat*. Before I read the story aloud, I pointed out the word *hat*. I told the students that we were going to be working with the word family *-at*, represented by the word *hat*. As I was reading the story, I paused when I came to an *-at* family word. I had students guess what the word would be. After we read the story aloud, I helped the students come up with as many *-at* words as we could. I wrote on chart paper the different words they said. Some of the words the students came up with were *at, bat, cat, fat, hat, mat, pat, rat, sat, flat, chat, that, catch, hatch, patch, matter,* and *platter*. Next, the students wrote their *-at* words on a hat made out of construction paper. We hung the hats on a bulletin board entitled "Aunt Lucy's Hats," to help the students remember the *-at* family.

PRACTICE: To practice with the *-at* family. I gave each student a highlighter and a copy of a poem entitled "That Cat!" by Jaime Lucero. I read it through to provide a fluent model and then the students read it aloud with me. Next, the students highlighted all of the *-at* words in the poem. The poem read:

That Cat!

That big fat cat

Sat on Aunt Pat's hat,

And now it's flat

As a welcome mat.

Now when Aunt Pat

Comes to sit and chat

She wears on her head

A big flat hat.

After the students highlighted all of the -*at* words, the students illustrated how they envisioned the poem.

REFLECT: To reflect, we discussed what made a word part of a word family. We also reviewed how to come up with words in a word family. Mark explained that he went down the alphabet and tried each letter with the word family to see if it made a word. If it didn't, he went to the next letter. He said, "I use the alphabet chart on top of the chalkboard to help me, so I don't skip any letters."

STAGE 2   Teacher-Guided Small-Group Instruction

TEXT: *Sheep in a Jeep* (Shaw, 1986)

REVIEW: To review, I reminded students what a word family was. I told the students that we were going to be working with a new word family after reading the book entitled *Sheep in a Jeep.* I asked the students what word family they thought we might be working with. Kevin said he thought it would be the *-eep* family because *-eep* was in both *sheep* and *jeep.*

GUIDE: I introduced the story and the students followed along as I read the book aloud. Each time we noticed an *-eep* word, the students made a beeping sound like a horn. We made a beeping sound because the word *beep* is in the *-eep* family. For example, when we came to the word *steep,* all of the students said, "beep, beep."

PRACTICE: When we finished reading the story aloud, the students created a sheep out of white construction paper and used their crayons to decorate the face. I cut two slits in the middle of their sheep and gave each student a long, skinny strip of paper that fit into the slits. The students wrote *eep* next to their slits. On the long skinny strip of paper, they wrote letters that could be put in front of *eep* to create a new word that fit into the *-eep* family. Before the students wrote on their strips of paper, I had them brainstorm different *-eep* words with me. We wrote them on chart paper. While brainstorming, students could refer back to their book *Sheep in a Jeep.* The different letters the students wrote on their strips of paper were *b, w, d, cr, j, sl, k, st, p, sw,* and *sh.* Next, we put the long slip of paper into their sheep. The students then pulled through the strip of paper to form new words. The students took turns reading their words to a partner. Kim's completed sheep is featured in Figure 3-4.

REFLECT: To reflect, we talked about how making new word-family words helped us to learn to use new words. Elizabeth said that it was easy to make the word-family words if we just thought about words that rhymed. We also discussed how much fun it was to learn *-eep* words with our sheep!

FIGURE 3-4

Student-Facilitated Centers

LISTENING CENTER: Students listened to the book *Down by the Cool of the Pool*, by Tony Mitton. Then they became word-family detectives. They went back into the text and looked for words that fit into the word families *-ool, -ee, -amp, -ound, -op, -ow, -ance, -ip,* and *-op* and recorded the words in their journals.

MAKING WORDS CENTER: Students worked in pairs. They chose word families from a mystery envelope and created as many words as they could using that word family. Any word family could be used for this activity, but we had been working with short-a word families, so I wrote *-ack, -ag, -ab, -ad, -am,* and *-an* on index cards and placed them in the mystery envelope. If time permitted, they chose a second card and made words using that family. Some students used their magnetic letters and cookie sheets to do this. Other students extended the activity to Making and Writing Words and wrote the words they created in their journals.

STAGE 3 Teacher-Facilitated Whole-Group Reflection

SHARE: The students shared and explained the work they completed in Stage 2. They shared with partners all of the words they found at the Listening Center and made at the Making Words Center that fit the different word families.

REFLECT: We reflected on how to create words using different word families, and how that helped us improve our reading, writing, and spelling. Jasmine said, "If we know the word families, we can make a lot of words!"

SET NEW GOALS: We decided to continue working with word families and applying what we learned to our reading, writing, and discussion.

Assessment Options

I reviewed and commented on the hats the students created and used a lot of observation during this lesson. I also checked the students' work from centers to make sure their words fit the different word families.

Final Thoughts on This Chapter

The lessons in this chapter integrated research findings and current beliefs about best practice in teaching phonics. The research-based Guided Comprehension Model for the Primary Grades provided a format that integrated direct and guided instruction as well as numerous opportunities for independent practice. Texts at a variety of levels and various modes of reader response were incorporated to accommodate students' abilities. Reflection and informal assessments permeated the lessons, which were designed to foster students' understanding of phonics.

It's important to note that although the lessons featured in this chapter were taught at a particular grade level, they can be adapted to accommodate other levels and needs. For example, these lessons were taught by first-grade teachers, but if kindergarten students are ready to begin learning phonics or if upper-grade students have not mastered phonics, the lessons can be used to teach them. Students develop at their own rates, and their needs for different skills and strategies vary. Ideas to adapt the lessons to accommodate English Language Learners, struggling readers, and special needs students include changing the level of the texts, adding more modeling and demonstration, providing more examples or focusing on fewer examples, providing time for more guided instruction or independent practice, and changing the level of word choice or questioning. Most of the lessons address skills and strategies that develop over time and continue to need reinforcement.

In the next chapter, we examine the role of fluency in the reading process. We begin by addressing its theoretical underpinnings and then present a variety of lessons focused on teaching fluency in the primary grades.

What can we read to learn more about teaching phonics?

Bear, D. R., Templeton, S., Invernizzi, M., & Johnston, F. (2003). *Words their way: Word study for phonics, vocabulary, and spelling* (3rd ed.). Upper Saddle River, NJ: Merrill/Prentice-Hall.

Cunningham, P. (2000). *Phonics they use: Words for reading and writing* (3rd ed.). New York: HarperCollins.

Stahl, S. A., Duffy-Hester, A. M., & Stahl, K. A. D. (1998). Theory and research in practice: Everything you wanted to know about phonics (but were afraid to ask). *Reading Research Quarterly, 33* (3), 338–355.

CHAPTER 4

Fluency

Fluency is enjoying a renaissance. After years of being left out of or barely mentioned in teaching of reading texts, fluency is now considered to be one of the five building blocks of literacy. And it should be. It is an essential component of literacy. Becoming fluent readers eliminates word-by-word reading and helps students to better comprehend what they read.

Helping our students to become fluent readers is the focus of this chapter. In Part One, we explain what fluency is, present what the research has to say, and discuss how to integrate the research results in our teaching. In Part Two, we present teacher-authored, classroom-tested, strategy-based Guided Comprehension lessons focused on different methods of promoting fluency. The chapter concludes with final thoughts and a short list of suggested readings.

Part One: Research Base

What is fluency?

Fluency is (1) the clear, easy, written or spoken expression of ideas; (2) freedom from word-identification problems that might hinder comprehension in silent reading or the expression of ideas in oral reading; (3) automaticity (Harris & Hodges, 1995, p. 85).

What does the research tell us?

According to Rasinski (2004), fluency builds a bridge to comprehension. The structure consists of accuracy in word decoding (sounding out words with minimal errors), automatic processing (using as little mental energy as possible to decode, so the energy can be used to comprehend), and prosodic reading (parsing the text into appropriate syntactic and semantic units). Samuels (2002) concurs, noting that becoming a fluent reader is challenging because components of reading, such as word recognition, determining the meaning of words, grouping words into grammatical units, generating inferences, and constructing meaning must be coordinated to happen simultaneously.

Oakley (2003) reports that fluent readers are more likely to read more and learn more, and, consequently, become even more fluent. In addition, Rasinski and Padak (2000) note that fluent readers have more positive attitudes toward reading and more positive concepts of themselves as readers.

It is generally agreed that fluency is an outcome of reading practice. Good reading models, teacher feedback, and methods such as repeated reading foster fluency, as do low-risk environments where students are comfortable and willing to read (Nathan & Stanovich, 1991).

To become fluent readers, students need to have good models, access to text, and time to read. To practice fluency, students engage in techniques such as choral reading and rereading of familiar texts. To do this independently, they need to have access to text that is easy to read. One of the many benefits of having leveled texts in classrooms is that students can read them to improve fluency.

How can we make the research-teaching connection?

Research indicates that using techniques such as repeated reading and Readers Theater in our teaching helps our students become more fluent readers. In Part Two of this chapter, we present strategy-based Guided Comprehension lessons that focus on fostering fluency. The lessons feature direct and guided instructions, as well as opportunities for independent practice in centers and routines; incorporate different genres at a variety of levels; and provide students with plenty of time to read, write, and discuss independently.

Part Two: Lesson Overview

In this chapter, all of the lessons focus on fluency. Featured texts include *If You Take a Mouse to School* (Numeroff, 2002); *If You Give a Pig a Pancake* (Numeroff, 1998); *A Pizza the Size of the Sun* (Prelutsky, 1994); *The Stinky Cheese Man and Other Fairly Stupid Tales* (Scieszka, 2002); *Squids Will Be Squids* (Scieszka, 1998); *Ride a Purple Pelican* (Prelutsky, 1986); *Tyrannosaurus Was a Beast* (Prelutsky, 1988); *Making Pancakes* (Pritchett, 2004); *At the Farmer's Market* (James, 2004); *Sharing a Pizza* (Griffiths, 2004); *Read-Aloud Rhymes for the Very Young* (Prelutsky, 1986); *Where's Your Smile, Crocodile?* (Freedman, 2001); *Wolf!* (Bloom, 1999); and *What's the Time, Grandma Wolf?* (Brown, 2001). Appendix A contains a list of additional texts that can be used for fluency instruction.

The lessons in this chapter are appropriate for all types of learners. In our classrooms we may have students who speak English as a second language, struggling readers, and students with special needs. To accommodate these learners, the lessons include the use of multiple modalities (singing, sketching, and so on), working with partners, books on tape, cross-age experiences, and extra guided instruction for students who struggle. For ideas on further adapting the lessons, see "Final Thoughts" at the end of the chapter.

This section features five teacher-authored, classroom-tested lessons that each address a specific aspect of teaching fluency: fluent reader models, echo reading, choral reading, repeated readings, and readers theater. (Descriptions of each of these activities can be found in Appendix E, p. 188.) The lessons feature teacher think-alouds and student work. They were designed using the Guided Comprehension Model for the Primary Grades (McLaughlin, 2003), which was discussed in Chapter 1.

LESSON 1   The Fluent Reading Model

STAGE 1   Teacher-Directed Whole-Group Instruction

TEXTS: "Mice," by Rose Fyleman, in *Read-Aloud Rhymes for the Very Young* (Prelutsky, 1986)

If You Take a Mouse to School (Numeroff, 2002)

EXPLAIN: I began by explaining to the students that to become good readers it is important to listen to other people read, especially better readers. I said, "When we listen to better readers, it helps us to know what we should sound like when we read." I pointed out that when we read, our sentences should flow and we should read with expression. I reminded them about different punctuation marks and how they provided clues to help us understand when and how long to pause while we are reading. To illustrate the difference between word-by-word reading and fluent reading, I read a few lines from our morning message in a word-by-word, choppy style. During this reading, I was careful to ignore all of the punctuation clues. Then I reread the morning message fluently and the students immediately noted that they could understand the second reading better. Then we discussed why they could understand it better. Their responses included "The words didn't keep on going"; "It was slower, but not too slow"; "You stopped sometimes"; "You made some words sound more important than others."

Next, I told the students that during our lesson they were going to be listening to me read a poem and a story, and I wanted them to pay close attention to how I read. I asked them to listen for three things: (1) how I read with expression; (2) how I used punctuation clues to create word flow, and (3) how I read at an appropriate rate. Then I explained that after they had listened to me read, they were going to practice reading so they could hear how they read with expression, how they used punctuation clues to create word flow, and how they read at an appropriate rate.

DEMONSTRATE: To demonstrate, I introduced and read to the students the poem entitled "Mice" by Rose Fyleman. I had written the poem on a transparency, which I placed on an overhead projector so that the children could follow along with me. The poem read:

> **Mice**
>
> I think mice
>
> Are rather nice.
>
> Their tails are long,
>
> Their faces small,
>
> They haven't any chins at all.
>
> Their ears are pink,
>
> Their teeth are white,
>
> They run about
>
> The house at night.
>
> They nibble things
>
> They shouldn't touch
>
> And no one seems
>
> To like them much.
>
> But I think mice
>
> Are nice.

As I read the poem to the students, I was careful to read with expression. I also pointed out places where I would pause because of the punctuation marks the author had used. I read at a viable rate—not too fast, not too slow. I read the poem three times. The first time I read it straight through to demonstrate how good readers read, the second time I paused and pointed out places I read with particular expression or paused, and the third time I again modeled how good readers read.

GUIDE: To guide the students, I read aloud the book *If You Take a Mouse to School*. I used a big book so that the children could follow along with me, and so I could point out places to use expression and where to pause for punctuation when reading. After introducing the book to the students, I read a few pages aloud and asked students to point out when I paused or changed expression. I continued doing this as I finished reading the story. Then we talked about the story and how listening to a fluent reading helped us to understand it.

PRACTICE: To practice, I invited the students to reread the book with me. I reminded them that good readers read at an appropriate pace, read with expression, and use punctuation clues to understand when to pause or stop reading. Then we read the book together. If the students needed more work on a certain sentence or page, we read it over again. After we finished reading the book, I put multiple copies of it in the reading corner so that students could use the book to practice fluent reading.

REFLECT: We reflected on the importance of reading with expression, using punctuation clues, and maintaining an appropriate reading rate. We discussed that fluent reading not only sounds better but also helps us understand and remember what we read. Jenelle said, "It's hard to understand what someone is reading when they read too slow." Evan said, "It's boring when people read without expression. I like when my mom reads to me with lots of different voices."

STAGE 2 Teacher-Guided Small-Group Instruction

TEXT: *If You Give a Pig a Pancake* (Numeroff, 1998)
(Texts varied according to students' abilities.)

REVIEW: To review, I reminded students about reading with expression, using punctuation clues, and maintaining an appropriate reading rate. I told the students that I was going to read them another story by Laura Numeroff, called *If You Give a Pig a Pancake*. They were to listen carefully to hear what a fluent reading sounds like.

GUIDE: To guide the students, I introduced and read aloud the book *If You Give a Pig a Pancake*. The students all had individual books to follow along with. At various points in the book, I would stop and have them reread a page with me so that I could hear their rate and expression. Then we discussed the story.

PRACTICE: To practice, I had the students read the story aloud to a partner using expression and fluent rate. I listened to each student read a few pages to his or her partner and noted any students who had difficulty. We continued to work on our fluency for the next few weeks. Students also practiced independently with books at easier levels.

REFLECT: The students noticed that when I read the story first, it was easier for them to read it fluently. They said that listening to me read it first gave them "good ideas" about how they should read it. They also pointed out that when they read and reread the same text, each reading sounded better. I explained to the students that reading something multiple times helps us to read more fluently because every reading helps us to become more familiar with the words and structure of the text.

Student-Facilitated Centers

LISTENING CENTER: Students listened to a reading of the book *If You Take a Mouse to the Movies* by Laura Numeroff. Then they took turns reading the book aloud to a partner to demonstrate their fluency.

AUTHOR CENTER: Students "read" wordless books, such as *Carl's Masquerade* by Alexandra Day. They began by previewing the books by "reading" the illustrations—looking at the illustrations on each page and using that information to understand what was happening in the story. Then the students used a tape recorder to tape themselves telling their version of the story. I reminded students that they should tell their story with expression, pause appropriately, and maintain an appropriate rate. I also explained to them that when we read or tell stories, it should sound just like when we speak during conversations. Later in the day, I listened to their stories on tape.

(STAGE 3) Teacher-Facilitated Whole-Group Reflection

SHARE: The students shared information about the wordless picture books they had "read." The students enjoyed listening to their classmates' stories.

REFLECT: We reflected on how reading fluently can help us become better readers. The students liked patterning their reading after fluent-reader models. At this point, I reminded the students that even though most of them knew how to read, they should still have family members read to them and with them at home so they would have good reading models. Tomás asked if that was why I read them a story aloud each day. I told him that it was one of the many reasons I read to them. The students all agreed that they enjoyed hearing stories read aloud. The students also wanted to continue practicing their reading so they could sound like the more experienced readers. Natalie said, "It's like my swimming lessons. When I learn how to do something, I do it over and over and it gets better every time."

SET NEW GOALS: Our goal was to continue to develop our fluency by reading and by listening to a lot of readers. We decided to invite parents and other family members to join in helping us reach our goal of becoming more fluent readers.

Assessment Options

I used observation and peer assessment of their reading to assess the students. If students continued to have difficulties reading with expression, pausing at punctuation clues, or reading at an appropriate rate, I continued working on these skills in small groups.

LESSON 2   Echo Reading

STAGE 1   Teacher-Directed Whole-Group Instruction

TEXTS: *A Pizza the Size of the Sun* (Prelutsky, 1994)

The Stinky Cheese Man and Other Fairly Stupid Tales
(Scieszka, 2002)

EXPLAIN: I explained to the students that they would
be echo-reading today. I explained what an echo was.
I told them it is like a parrot when it repeats whatever you say. To ensure that they understood, I pretended I was a parrot and echoed whatever they said. Then I explained to the
students that they were going to follow along as I read a passage aloud. Next, they would
echo what I read. Finally, they would read with a partner, trying to read the passage just
as I had, using the same pace and expression.

DEMONSTRATE: To demonstrate, I read "Spaghetti Seeds" by Jack Prelutsky. I put the
poem on a transparency on the overhead projector. First, I introduced the poem and read
it through to provide a fluent model. Next, I read the first two lines aloud and asked the
students to echo my reading. We continued this process until we had read the entire
poem. I stopped to explain the punctuation for the students so that they would know why
I paused or changed my expression. Finally, each of them read the poem aloud to a partner,
and we discussed the poem.

GUIDE: To guide the students, I introduced them to the book entitled *The Stinky Cheese
Man and Other Fairly Stupid Tales*. I told them they were going to echo-read one of the
tales in the book with me. I put "The Ugly Ducking" on overhead transparencies so that
all the students could see it in order to echo-read. Then I read the tale to provide a fluent
model. After reading, I pointed out that the letters on the last page are really big. I asked
the students why they thought Jon Scieszka formatted it that way. They said that when I
read that part, I read it louder and made it sound important, so they thought that was
why the author had it printed that way. During the second reading, the students echoed my
reading, paying particular attention to phrasing and punctuation clues. Students engaged in
partner reading for the third reading. This time they took turns echoing each other. I
monitored this part of the lesson by writing observational notes about various students.

PRACTICE: To practice, I assigned each student a partner who was at approximately the same reading level. I gave each pair a copy of a poem by Jack Prelutsky. I tried to give poems to the students that were appropriate for their reading levels. The students practiced echo-reading the poems. Then each partner read it through, giving his best effort.

REFLECT: To reflect, we discussed that echo reading helps us to practice our expression, pay attention to punctuation clues, and read at an appropriate rate. I explained that they could also echo-read with their third-grade cross-age buddies.

STAGE 2 Teacher-Guided Small-Group Instruction

TEXT: *Squids Will Be Squids* (Scieszka, 1998)
(Texts varied according to students' abilities.)

REVIEW: To review, I asked the students to tell me what an echo is. Shavonda replied, "It is when you repeat what someone says." I told them that they would be echo-reading with me. I asked them to pay close attention to my expression, use of punctuation clues, and the rate at which I was reading. I asked them to echo my reading of paragraphs as closely as they could.

GUIDE: To guide the students, I introduced and read them the tale "Elephant & Mouse" from the book *Squids Will Be Squids*. Each student had a copy of the book to follow along. I stopped after each paragraph to have the students echo-read. In the tale, there is a line that is entirely in uppercase letters. I explained to the students that this line really needed to be stressed. As I read the paragraphs, they echoed. I moved around the table so that I could listen to each student read.

PRACTICE: To practice, I assigned each student a partner to echo-read with. Together, they echo-read two more tales from the book. I listened to each pair. Then we discussed the stories they had read so that everyone would hear about the different tales.

REFLECT: To reflect, we discussed how fluent reading helps us to comprehend better. I reminded the students that when we read we need to notice the clues the author gives us, such as the different punctuation marks and different sizes and styles of print. The students enjoyed hearing all of the different tales and morals.

Student-Facilitated Center and Routine

LISTENING CENTER: Students listened to the book *Does a Kangaroo Have a Mother, Too?* by Eric Carle. The students pushed the pause button after each page and echoed the reader on the tape. After they had finished echo-reading the book, they read the book quietly.

CROSS-AGE READING EXPERIENCES: Students echo-read books from their book baskets with their third-grade reading buddies. I stressed to the third graders that they should use lots of expression as they read, pay close attention to the punctuation, and read at an appropriate rate. After echo-reading, the students discussed the stories and sketched the most interesting scenes.

(STAGE 3) Teacher-Facilitated Whole-Group Reflection

SHARE: Students shared their sketches and talked in small groups about their echo reading at the centers and in their Cross-Age Reading Experiences.

REFLECT: Students reflected on how echo reading helps them become better readers. They noticed that if they listened first and followed along with the reader, it helped them to know what kind of expression to use, how to respond to punctuation clues, and how to read at an appropriate rate.

SET NEW GOALS: We decided to continue our quest to become more fluent readers by using tape recorders, so we could listen to ourselves read and set new goals to improve our fluency.

Assessment Options

I used observation to assess students' fluency. I wrote notes about various students and how I could continue to help them with their fluency.

LESSON 3 Choral Reading

STAGE 1 Teacher-Directed Whole-Group Instruction

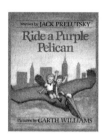

TEXT: *Ride a Purple Pelican* (Prelutsky, 1986)

EXPLAIN: I explained to the students that we would be reading aloud together some poetry by Jack Prelutsky. I explained that I wanted them to read the poems or stories with me, trying to use the same expression and pace I did. I said, "Good readers change their voices to make the passage sound more interesting. They also pay attention to clues from the author and read at appropriate rates."

DEMONSTRATE: To demonstrate, I had the students write a "today" story with me. We do this every morning, to practice our writing and reading skills. When we finish writing the story together we always read it chorally. This is the story we wrote today:

> Today is Monday. The weather is rainy and cold. We will be reading
> with our reading buddies this morning. This afternoon, we have gym
> and art. We will be learning about different dinosaurs in science.
> Today will be a great day!

After the students helped me write the story on chart paper, we read the story chorally, using expression and paying attention to punctuation and reading rate.

GUIDE: To guide the students, I explained that we would be chorally reading a few poems from *Ride a Purple Pelican,* just as we had done with the today story. I put the poems on overheads, so that all of the students could see the words. I explained to the students that we would first whisper-read the poem. Then we would read the poem chorally focusing on using the same expression, attention to punctuation, and rate that I used. When we finished reading the first poem, I pointed out the commas and the punctuation marks and reminded the students of what we do when we see those marks. Then we read the poem again. It worked out better the second time, and we followed this procedure with three more poems.

PRACTICE: To practice, I gave each table of four students two different poems from *Ride a Purple Pelican*. Each student had a copy of the poems. Each group of students practiced chorally reading their poems and then read them to the class. I reminded them that they should all be reading together and with expression. I gave them some time to practice together. Then they shared their poems with the class and we discussed them.

REFLECT: To reflect, we discussed how much better the poems sounded when we read with tone and expression and practiced reading several times. They all agreed that they had read much better the second or third time they read their poems together.

(STAGE 2) Teacher-Guided Small-Group Instruction

TEXT: *Tyrannosaurus Was a Beast* (Prelutsky, 1988)
(Texts varied according to students' abilities.)

REVIEW: To review, I reminded the students that we would be practicing reading chorally in our small group. I explained that we would be reading poems about different kinds of dinosaurs, written by Jack Prelutsky. We were in the middle of a dinosaur theme, so these poems fit perfectly.

GUIDE: To guide the students, I read a poem about a tyrannosaurus, making sure I used good expression and pacing. During the second reading, the students and I read the poem chorally. Then we followed the same process with another poem, entitled "Brachiosaurus."

PRACTICE: To practice, I had the students read the rest of the dinosaur poems chorally as a small group. When I noticed the students were having difficulty, I had them reread the poem. I also gave the students clues as to whether they should slow down, speed up, pause, show more expression, and so on.

REFLECT: To reflect, we discussed the importance of our fluency and expression as we read. I had students volunteer to read one poem aloud to the group if they wished. Most students volunteered to do this. I think they felt comfortable reading in front of the group because they had practiced chorally.

Student-Facilitated Centers

POETRY CENTER: Students read poems from Jack Prelutsky books chorally with a partner or small group that was at approximately the same reading level. They then chose their favorite poem and recorded themselves reading it aloud. We listened to the poems as a class in Stage 3.

LISTENING CENTER: Students could choose from several different books on tape that they had read before. They read with the tape quietly, trying to use the same expression and fluency as the reader on the tape.

(STAGE 3) Teacher-Facilitated Whole-Group Reflection

SHARE: Students discussed poems they had read chorally with a partner or small group in the centers. Then we played the tape and listened to everyone read his or her favorite poems. The students enjoyed listening to themselves as they read.

REFLECT: To reflect, we once again discussed how listening and reading with other fluent readers helps us to become better readers.

SET NEW GOALS: We decided to continue to improve our fluency by extending our choral reading to informational texts.

Assessment Options

I used observation and the audiotape of students' reading to assess.

LESSON 4 Repeated Reading

STAGE 1 Teacher-Directed Whole-Group Instruction

 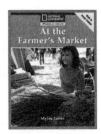

TEXTS: *Making Pancakes* (Pritchett, 2004)

At the Farmer's Market (James, 2004)

Sharing a Pizza (Griffiths, 2004)

EXPLAIN: I explained to the students that we would be reading a book entitled *Making Pancakes*. I explained that we would be reading it several times to help us improve our fluency. I told the students that the more we read a book or passage, the more fluently we will read it and the better we will comprehend it. I explained that we were going to read *Making Pancakes*, a short book, several times. First, I would read it. Next, we would chorally read it. Finally, they would read it twice for their partner and the partner would comment on how well it had been read. Then they would change roles.

DEMONSTRATE: To demonstrate, I wrote a paragraph on chart paper about my favorite food: pizza. Then I read the paragraph aloud to the students. Next, we chorally read it. Then each partner read it twice to the other, offering comments and suggestions. Finally, we discussed pizza and talked about how reading the same text multiple times helped us to read more fluently.

GUIDE: To guide the students, I read aloud the big book *Making Pancakes*. I chose a very short, easy book to start with. Then we read the book chorally. Finally, each student read it twice to his or her partner, each offering comments and suggestions to the other. I listened as the partners read, offering my own suggestions as needed.

PRACTICE: To practice, I paired a more able reader with a less able reader and gave them the books *At the Farmer's Market* and *Sharing a Pizza*. The students took turns being the teacher and the student. They read the short books in the same ways we had earlier. They each read the book four times. The students helped each other if they had any difficulties. Then they discussed the stories.

REFLECT: To reflect, we talked about how each successive reading became easier and easier. The students enjoyed having someone to offer positive comments and suggestions.

STAGE 2 Teacher-Guided Small-Group Instruction

TEXTS: *Read-Aloud Rhymes for the Very Young* (Prelutsky, 1986)

Where's Your Smile, Crocodile? (Freedman, 2001)

(Texts varied according to students' abilities.)

REVIEW: To review, I reminded the students that repeated reading helps us to become more fluent and able readers. I explained to the students that we would be reading a poem and a story using repeated readings.

GUIDE: To guide the students, I presented them with copies of a poem entitled "Someone's Face," by John Ciardi. The poem was from Jack Prelutsky's book *Read-Aloud Rhymes for the Very Young*. I read the poem the first time while the students followed along. Then we chorally read the poem. Next, they read the poem twice to their partners. Finally they read the poem aloud to me, and we discussed it.

PRACTICE: To practice, I assigned each student a partner. I gave them each a copy of the book *Where's Your Smile, Crocodile?* We briefly discussed the title and cover illustration. Ahead of time, I placed sticky notes on four pages in the books. The students engaged in partner reading and when they came to a sticky note, they used Repeated Reading. They read the marked passage four times, two times each, offering comments and suggestion as needed. After they had read the book, we discussed the story.

REFLECT: To reflect, students talked about how they had helped their partners. Luis said that he had reminded his partner to pause just a little at a comma. Renee shared that she had reminded her partner to read with more expression when the words were in all capital letters. Overall, the students' repeated readings worked very well.

Student-Facilitated Centers

LISTENING CENTER: Students worked with partners and listened to a variety of books. They paused the tape after each page and read quietly, but still aloud, the page that had just been read. They did this throughout the book, stopping to engage in Repeated Reading at least twice.

PARTNER READING CENTER: Students were assigned partners. They chose poems to read from *Read-Aloud Rhymes for the Very Young*. As they read the poems, they used Repeated Reading.

(**STAGE 3**) Teacher-Facilitated Whole-Group Reflection

SHARE: The students shared what they learned from their various Repeated Reading experiences.

REFLECT: The students truly appreciated being able to read independently and help each other during the repeated readings. Henri said that it was like being a teacher and a student all at once. He got to help his partner and his partner helped him. Students agreed the best part was the final time they read the text during Repeated Reading. They said that was great because they read it so well by then.

SET NEW GOALS: Students decided that when they didn't have a partner, they could help themselves by reading some pages more than once and focusing on their expression, author clues, and rate. So we decided to investigate a different way of partner reading next: Readers Theater.

Assessment Options

I primarily used observation to assess.

LESSON 5 Readers Theater

STAGE 1 Teacher-Directed Whole-Group Instruction

TEXT: *Wolf!* (Bloom, 1999)

EXPLAIN: I explained to the students that we would be reading a story using a method called Readers Theater. I said, "Readers Theater is like putting on a play, but we don't have to memorize lines, make props, or set up a stage." I told the students that they would use their reading voices to help develop the characters and to make the story come alive using only the spoken words.

DEMONSTRATE: To demonstrate, I had the children help me develop a short dialogue that takes place between a teacher and a student about the student forgetting to do homework. This is the dialogue we wrote:

Teacher:	Russ, it seems that I am missing your homework from last night.
Russ:	I, I thought I put it in the pile this morning.
Teacher:	Why don't you go look in your backpack?
Russ:	I looked, but it is not there.
Teacher:	Are you sure you did it?
Russ:	Well, I think my baby sister got hold of it.
Teacher:	Russ, you don't have a baby sister.
Russ:	Or maybe my dog ate it.
Teacher:	Your dog? What kind of dog do you have?
Russ:	A, uh, German poodle.
Teacher:	Russ, tell me the truth. Did you forget to do your homework?
Russ:	Yes, I'm sorry. Can I bring it in tomorrow?
Teacher:	Of course, but next time, please just tell me the truth.

I had a student read the script with me and we both used a lot of expression. I told the students to visualize the situation happening by just listening to the dialogue between us. The students closed their eyes and listened to our voices. I explained that simply by using our voices, we could make an audience imagine and feel what was happening.

GUIDE: To guide the students, I told them we would be using Readers Theater to read the book entitled *Wolf!* by Becky Bloom. I had gone through the text and turned the book into characters' lines. I said, "There are a few different characters, such as a narrator, the wolf, a duck, a pig, and a cow. Before we decide who will have which part, I am going to introduce the story and read it aloud to you, so you will know what it is about." After I read the story aloud, I placed the students in groups of five. Each group practiced reading the story using the Readers Theater script. The students decided which character's part they wanted to read.

PRACTICE: To practice, the students read their scripts with their groups using a lot of expression to try to bring the story to life. The following is the script the students used for the book *Wolf!*:

Script adapted from *Wolf!* by Becky Bloom

Narrator: After walking for many days, a wolf wandered into a quiet little town. He was tired and hungry, his feet ached, and he had only a little money that he kept for emergencies. Then he remembered.

Wolf: There's a farm outside this village. I'll find some food there.

Narrator: As he peered over the farm fence, he saw a pig, a duck, and a cow reading in the sun.

Wolf: I have never seen animals read before. I'm so hungry that my eyes are playing tricks on me.

Narrator: But the wolf was very hungry and didn't stop to think about it for long. The wolf stood up tall, took a deep breath, and leaped at the animals with a howl.

Wolf: AaaOOOOOooo!

Narrator: Chickens and rabbits ran for their lives, but the duck, the pig, and the cow didn't budge.

Cow: What is that awful noise? I can't concentrate on my book.

Duck: Just ignore it.

Narrator: The wolf did not like to be ignored.

Wolf: What's wrong with you? Can't you see I'm a big and dangerous wolf?

Pig: I'm sure you are, but couldn't you be big and dangerous somewhere else? We're trying to read. This is a farm for educated animals. Now be a good wolf and go away.

Narrator: The wolf had never been treated like this before.

Wolf: Educated animals... educated animals! This is something new. Well then! I'll learn how to read too.

Narrator: Off he went to school. The children found it strange to have a wolf in their class, but since he didn't try to eat anyone, they soon got used to him. The wolf was serious and hardworking, and after much effort he learned to read and write. Soon he became the best in class. Feeling quite satisfied, the wolf went back to the farm and jumped over the fence.

Wolf: I'll show them.

Narrator: He opened his book and began to read.

Wolf: Run, wolf! Run! See wolf run.

Duck: You've got a long way to go.

Narrator: The pig, the duck, and the cow went on reading their own books, not the least impressed. The wolf jumped back over the fence and ran straight to the public library. He studied long and hard, reading lots of dusty old books, and he practiced until he could read without stopping.

Wolf: They'll be impressed with my reading now.

Narrator: The wolf walked up to the farm gate and knocked. He opened *The Three Little Pigs* and began to read:

Wolf: Onceuponatimetherewerethreelittlepigsonedaytheir mothercalledthemandtoldthem—

Duck: Stop that racket!

Pig: You've improved, but you still need to work on your style.

Narrator: The wolf tucked his tail between his legs and slunk away. But the wolf wasn't about to give up. He counted the little money he had left, went to the book shop, and bought a splendid new storybook. His first very own book!

Wolf: I'm going to read this book day and night, every letter and every line. I will read so well that the farm animals will admire me.

Narrator: Ding-dong, rang the wolf at the farm gate. He lay down on the grass, made himself comfortable, took out his new book, and began to read. He read with confidence and passion, and the pig, the cow, and the duck all listened and said not one word. Each time he finished a story, the pig, the duck, and the cow asked if he would please read them another story. So the wolf read on, story after story. One minute he was Little Red Riding Hood, the next a genie emerging from a lamp, and then a swashbuckling pirate.

Duck: This is so much fun!

Pig: He's a master.

Cow: Why don't you join us on our picnic today?

Narrator: And so they all had a picnic—the pig, the duck, the cow, and the wolf. They lay in the tall grass and told stories all afternoon long.

Cow: We should all become storytellers.

Duck: We could travel around the world.

Pig: We can start tomorrow morning.

Narrator: The wolf stretched in the grass. He was happy to have such
            wonderful friends.

REFLECT: To reflect, the students discussed the script as a whole class. The students offered suggestions to help the script come to life even more. Many thought it would be helpful to have the students wear a headband or sign that would tell which character they were. I told the students I would give them time during art to make a mask or a sign to wear. Then they could practice their scripts again. We later performed Readers Theater in the other primary classrooms. Each group went to a different class to share the story.

STAGE 2 Teacher-Guided Small-Group Instruction

TEXT: *What's the Time, Grandma Wolf?* (K. Brown, 2001)
(Texts varied according to students' abilities.)

REVIEW: To review, I asked students to explain what Readers Theater is. Sarah responded by saying, "It is when we read a story like a play. Different people read the parts of the different characters." Andrew added, "We use our voices to bring the story to life." I reminded the students that they would not be moving around the room and acting out the scenes, but rather, they would be seated at their tables, using their voices to dramatize the story.

GUIDE: To guide the students, I read them the story *What's the Time, Grandma Wolf?* I then assigned parts to the students. The characters were Grandma Wolf, Piglet, Fawn, Crow, Squirrel, Badger, Duckling, Rabbit, and the Narrator. I had only five students in each small group, so each student read two parts, except for the student who read for Grandma Wolf.

PRACTICE: To practice, the students read the following script for *What's the Time, Grandma Wolf?*

Script adapted from *What's the Time, Grandma Wolf?*
by Ken Brown

Everyone: There's a wolf in the woods. She's big and she's bad, she's old and she's hairy. Best leave her alone, she's mean and she's scary.

Narrator: But they wanted to know, so they crept a bit closer, and Piglet, who's brave, shouted . . .

Piglet: What's the time, Grandma Wolf?

Narrator: She opened her eyes—they were very, very big—and she yawned.

Grandma Wolf: It's time I got up.

Narrator: So they crept a bit closer, and Fawn, who's shy, whispered . . .

Fawn: What's the time, Grandma Wolf?

Grandma Wolf: It's time I brushed my teeth.

Narrator: So they crept a bit closer, and Crow, who is noisy, squawked . . .

Crow: What's the time, Grandma Wolf?

Narrator: She took down a kettle and said,

Grandma Wolf: It's time I scrubbed the stewpot.

Narrator: So they crept a bit closer, and Squirrel, who's sassy, squeaked . . .

Squirrel: What's the time, Grandma Wolf?

Narrator: She fetched a sharp axe that was very big and said . . .

Grandma Wolf: It's time to chop the wood.

Narrator:	So we crept a bit closer, and Badger, who's bold, barked...
Badger:	What's the time, Grandma Wolf?
Narrator:	She picked up two pails that were very, very big, and said...
Grandma Wolf:	It's time I fetched some water.
Narrator:	So they crept a bit closer, and Duckling, who's silly, quacked...
Duckling:	What's the time, Grandma Wolf?
Narrator:	She looked down her nose that was very, very big, and said...
Grandma Wolf:	It's time to light the fire!
Narrator:	So they crept even closer, and Rabbit, who's reckless, giggled...
Rabbit:	What's the time, Grandma Wolf?
Grandma Wolf:	It's DINNERTIME!
Narrator:	So they all settled down to a vegetable stew, and old Grandma Wolf read them their favorite story!

REFLECT: To reflect, the students discussed how they could make their Readers Theater for *What's the Time, Grandma Wolf?* better. They decided they could talk in the style of each animal and demonstrate the characteristic of that animal. For example, it said the duck was silly and she quacked. Another idea was for Grandma Wolf to look ferocious as she read her lines, to make the story more believable and to make everyone think she was going to eat the animals. Once the reflections were complete, we reread the script.

Student-Facilitated Center

READERS THEATER CENTER: In groups of three, students read various scripts left at the center. The students decided what parts they would read. The scripts I used at the center were found on the Web site www.readerstheatre.ecsd.net. Other Readers Theater scripts can also be found online; another good source I used for scripts was www.teaching heart.net/readerstheater.htm

(STAGE 3) Teacher-Facilitated Whole-Group Reflection

REFLECT: Students reflected on how Readers Theater helped them to become more fluent readers and how very much they enjoyed engaging in it. Many of them thought that hearing different people's voices used for different characters really brought the books to life. They all agreed that it was important to use expression as they read and that it was also important to practice reading the scripts. Shana asked, "When can we turn another story into a Readers Theater? That was fun!" The other students agreed.

SET NEW GOALS: We decided that we would continue to use Readers Theater to improve our fluency by reading other scripts and presenting selected scripts for other classes.

Assessment Options

I used observation and audiotapes of students' participation in Readers Theater to assess during this lesson.

Final Thoughts on This Chapter

The lessons in this chapter integrated research findings and current beliefs about best practice in teaching fluency. The research-based Guided Comprehension Model for the Primary Grades provided a format that integrated direct and guided instruction as well as numerous opportunities for independent practice. Texts at a variety of levels and various modes of reader response were incorporated to accommodate students' abilities. Reflection and informal assessments permeated the lessons, which were designed to foster students' understanding of fluency.

It's important to note that although the lessons featured in this chapter were taught at particular grade levels, they can be adapted to accommodate other levels and needs. For example, these lessons were taught by first- (Lessons 1 and 2), second- (Lessons 3 and 4), and third-grade teachers (Lesson 5), but they are easily adaptable for use as read-alouds with kindergarten students or to teach upper-grade students who have not mastered fluency. Students develop at their own rates and their needs for different skills and strategies vary. Fluency lessons are most easily adapted by just changing the text level. Other ideas to adapt the lessons to accommodate English Language Learners, struggling readers, and special needs students include adding more modeling and demonstration, providing more examples or focusing on fewer examples, providing time for more guided instruction or independent practice, and changing the level of word choice or questioning. Most of the lessons address skills and strategies that develop over time and continue to need reinforcement.

In the next chapter, we examine the role of vocabulary in the reading process. We begin by addressing its theoretical underpinnings and then present a variety of lessons focused on teaching vocabulary in the primary grades.

What can we read to learn more about teaching fluency?

Rasinski, T. V. (2003). *The fluent reader*. New York: Scholastic.

Rasinski, T. V. (2004). Creating fluent readers. *Educational Leadership, 61* (6), 46–51.

Richards, M. (2000). Be a good detective: Solve the case of oral reading fluency. *The Reading Teacher, 53* (7), 534–539.

CHAPTER 5

Vocabulary

What we know about teaching and learning vocabulary has changed significantly in recent years. Most of us can remember endlessly writing definitions of the words on our vocabulary lists, but we now know that students need to do much more than write a word's definition in order to make the word part of their working vocabularies. They need to talk about words, take ownership of them, and use them in a variety of contexts.

According to Asselin (2002), students learn between 2,500 and 3,000 new words every year. If we want our students to actively use these words, we need to motivate them to understand how words work. Graves and Watts-Taffe (2002, p. 144) describe this as "word consciousness—the awareness of and interest in words and their meanings."

That's the focus of this chapter: helping students to develop an interest in words. In Part One, we explain what vocabulary is, present what the research has to say, and discuss how to integrate the research results into our teaching. In Part Two, we present teacher-authored, classroom-tested, strategy-based Guided Comprehension lessons for teaching vocabulary. The chapter concludes with final thoughts and a short list of suggested readings.

Part One: Research Base

What is vocabulary?

"Vocabulary is a list of words." Vocabulary development is "(1) the growth of a person's stock of known words and meanings; (2) the teaching-learning principles and practices that lead to such growth, as comparing and classifying word meanings, using context, analyzing root words and affixes, etc." (Harris & Hodges, 1995, p. 275)

What does the research tell us?

Themes that have emerged from research on vocabulary include the following:

- Vocabulary development and instruction play significant roles in students' reading comprehension.

- Reading widely enhances students' vocabulary.

- Repeated exposure to words helps students learn how to use them.

Professional development in teaching vocabulary and comprehension strategies and in helping students develop and use vocabulary is linked to student achievement. Both direct instruction and the use of context clues have been found to be effective in teaching vocabulary. Lessons that feature direct and guided instruction, as well as independent practice in a variety of settings, are featured in Part Two of this chapter. The lessons focus on the comprehension strategy knowing how words work. Research reports that knowing and using vocabulary-related strategies contribute to students' reading comprehension (Blachowicz & Fisher, 2000; National Reading Panel, 2000).

The overarching conclusion of the research on vocabulary is that it affects students' comprehension. This is logical if we consider that we cannot comprehend if we don't know what the words mean. Vocabulary instruction leads to gains in comprehension, but the methods must be appropriate to the age and ability of the reader. Students need to actively use the words—read them, hear them, write them, and speak them—in order for them to become part of their working vocabularies. Learning in rich contexts, having a wide variety of experiences, and using technology all facilitate students' acquisition of vocabulary.

How can we make the research-teaching connection?

Research supports students' using strategies to learn vocabulary. Consequently, our teaching the strategies will enhance our students' learning. In Part Two of this chapter, we present strategy-based Guided Comprehension lessons that focus on teaching techniques that engender appreciation for vocabulary and foster its development. The lessons feature direct and guided instruction as well as opportunities for independent practice in centers and routines; incorporate different genres at a variety of levels; and provide students with plenty of time to read, write, and discuss independently.

Part Two: Lesson Overview

In this chapter, all of the lessons focus on vocabulary. Featured texts are *The Little Red Hen Makes a Pizza* (Sturges, 1999); *Pancakes, Pancakes!* (Carle, 1991); *The Very Hungry Caterpillar* (Carle, 1981); *The Very Busy Spider* (Carle, 1989); *Nature's Green Umbrella* (Gibbons, 1997); *Save the Rain Forests* (Fowler, 1997); *Whales* (Gibbons, 1991); and *Wolves* (Simon, 1993).

The lessons in this chapter are appropriate for all types of learners. In our classrooms we may have students who speak English as a second language, struggling readers, and students with special needs. To accommodate these learners, the lessons include the use of multiple modalities (singing, sketching, and so on), working with partners, listening to books on tape, cross-age experiences, and extra guided instruction for students who struggle. For ideas on further adapting the lessons, see the "Final Thoughts" at the end of the chapter.

This section features teacher-authored, classroom-tested lessons that address specific techniques for teaching vocabulary and helping students take ownership of it. Teaching ideas include Concept of Definition Maps, Semantic Maps, Semantic Question Maps, Synonym Rhymes, and Vocabulary Bookmark Technique. Descriptions of each technique and related blackline masters can be found in Appendix F (p. 189). All of the lessons feature student work and were designed using the Guided Comprehension Model for the Primary Grades (McLaughlin, 2003), which was discussed in Chapter 1.

LESSON 1 Semantic Maps

TEXT: *The Little Red Hen Makes a Pizza* (Sturges, 1999)

EXPLAIN: I explained that knowing how words work helps us to understand the words we read; then I focused on the Semantic Map. I said, "Thinking about what we already know about words helps us to make connections to the words we read. We use Semantic Maps to show what we know about a particular focus word. We can record our thinking in categories on the map and summarize what we know about the focus word. That helps us to remember what the word means."

DEMONSTRATE: I used a posterboard and a think-aloud to demonstrate how to use a Semantic Map (see Appendix F, pp. 208-209). I showed a Semantic Map I had drawn on posterboard, pointed to the center oval, and said, "I am going to write a word inside this oval and then I am going to think about what I know about that word." Then I wrote *pizza* inside the oval. The children were very pleased with my word choice. Next, I said, "Now I need to think about what I know about

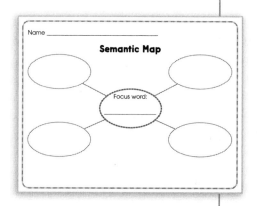

pizza. Can you help me? What do you know about pizza?" As students offered their suggestions, I recorded them on the board. After everyone offered an idea, I said, "Next, I need to think about what categories our responses fit into. For example, I see some of our responses were *pepperoni*, *mushroom*, *sausage*, and *extra cheese*. So, I need to think of a category those answers will fit into. I think the category they will fit into is 'kinds of pizza,' so I am going to write that on our Semantic Map." I pointed to the map and wrote "kinds of pizza" in the upper left side oval. Then I showed the students how we could list the kinds of pizza just below that oval. I put a line through each kind of pizza on the board as I added it to the Semantic Map.

GUIDE: To guide students, I said, "I wonder what other category we might find in our list of responses." I read these words from our list: *flour*, *dough*, *tomatoes*, *sauce*, and *cheese*, and the students responded, "What pizza is made of." I wrote what they said in the upper-right-side oval and asked them what pizza is made of. As students read the list of ingredients, I recorded them below the oval and put a line through each of them on the board. We completed the next oval after I read *Pizza Hut*, *Domino's*, *Pappas Pizza*, *Sal's Pizza*, and *Roma's Pizza* and the children suggested "places that make pizza" as the category.

PRACTICE: Students practiced by working in small groups to determine a final category. The words that were left were *cafeteria*, *home*, *football games*, *roller-skating*, and *basketball games*. Their responses were worded differently, but they agreed the category would be "places we eat pizza." I wrote that in last, and listed the words underneath it. We talked about what we knew about the word *pizza*. Sam said, "We know a lot more than I thought." Julie said, "When I think of pizza, I just think about pepperoni because that's the kind I like. But we know a lot of things about pizza." Then we read our Semantic Map aloud, creating an informal oral summary of "pizza." Next, I introduced and read aloud *The Little Red Hen Makes a Pizza*. As we discussed the book, we thought about connections we could make between this story and the original story of the Little Red Hen and between our completed Semantic Map and the book. Students noticed that the Little Red Hen worked alone in both stories. They also noticed that in *The Little Red Hen Makes a Pizza*, Duck, Cat, and Dog eat the pizza with Little Red Hen and do the dishes. When we were making connections between our Semantic Map and *Little Red Hen Makes a Pizza*, Jerry said, "On our map, we have different kinds of pizza. It doesn't talk about kinds of pizza in the book, but the pictures show all the toppings." Melanie said, "And on our map we had people who make pizza and Little Red Hen made pizza." Figure 5-1 features our completed Semantic Map.

REFLECT: We talked about how making a Semantic Map helps us understand words and how that helps us to understand what we read. I explained that we knew a lot about pizza, so we were able to complete our Semantic Map, but if the focus word ever was a word we didn't know a lot about, we could write what we knew on the map, read the text, and then add to the map the information we learned from reading. Abby said, "It was good to work with a word from the story before we heard the story. Talking about the word helped me know the story better." Finally, we talked about how we could use a Semantic Map in our small groups.

FIGURE 5-1

Semantic Map: Pizza

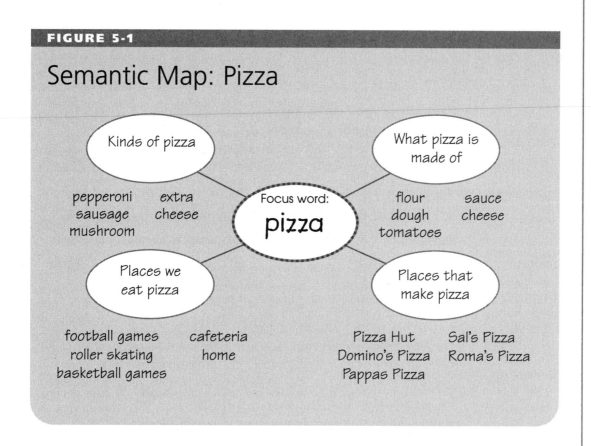

STAGE 2   Teacher-Guided Small-Group Instruction

TEXT: *Pancakes, Pancakes!* (Carle, 1991)

(Texts varied according to students' abilities.)

REVIEW: I reviewed the importance of knowing how words work and focused on using Semantic Maps. I reminded the students that Semantic Maps allow us to make connections between our background knowledge and the focus word, so we can understand the focus word more fully. I introduced *Pancakes, Pancakes!* and asked the students what they thought the focus word for our Semantic Map would be. They all responded, "Pancakes!"

GUIDE: They took turns recording information on our poster-size Semantic Map. Alison wrote "pancakes" in the oval marked "focus word." Because we were working in a small group, I had written a category in each of the extending ovals. The first oval read "Kinds of pancakes." Students responded, "blueberry, strawberry, chocolate chip, banana, and plain." Louis recorded these responses on our map. The second oval said "What pancakes are made of." The students replied, "eggs, milk, flour, sugar, butter, salt," and Nicky wrote their responses on the Semantic Map. The next category was "Places that serve pancakes." Students responded, "Perkins, Friendly's, and Waffle House." The final category was "People who make pancakes." The students responded, "cooks, Mom, Dad, Grandma, Grandpa, aunts, and uncles," and Lilly recorded them on our Semantic Map.

PRACTICE: We discussed our completed map (see Figure 5-2) and I guided the students in their reading of *Pancakes, Pancakes!* As they read about how Jack gathered the ingredients to make the pancakes he wanted for breakfast, I listened to the students whisper-read when I sat next to each of them. This gave me an opportunity to informally assess their fluency.

REREAD, RETELL, AND REFLECT: While the partner read the text, I completed a running record with one of the students. Then we engaged in an oral retelling. Finally, we reflected on knowing how words work and how using Semantic Maps help us make connections between what we know and what we are reading.

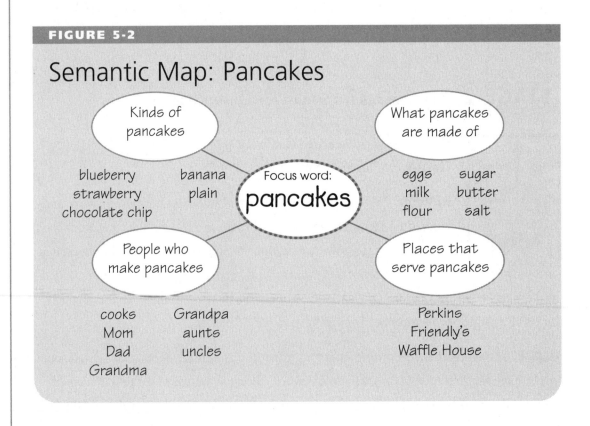

FIGURE 5-2

Semantic Map: Pancakes

Kinds of pancakes

What pancakes are made of

blueberry   banana
strawberry   plain
chocolate chip

Focus word:
pancakes

eggs   sugar
milk   butter
flour   salt

People who make pancakes

Places that serve pancakes

cooks   Grandpa
Mom   aunts
Dad   uncles
Grandma

Perkins
Friendly's
Waffle House

Student-Facilitated Centers and Routine

DRAMA CENTER: I placed a variety of puppets at this center, including a hen, a duck, a cat, and a dog. I also provided "pizza props," including plastic ingredients, and plastic dinnerware. Students used the puppets and props to use the language of the story to retell it.

THEME CENTER: I placed a variety of books—both published and student authored— about foods in the theme center. I was careful to include books about a lot of different foods as well as titles that represented a variety of genres and reading levels. I made sure that there were Semantic Map blacklines, complete with focus words and categories available for each book. Students worked with partners to complete the Semantic Map before reading the book. After reading the book, students discussed the book with their partners. They also had the option of revisiting their Semantic Maps to add information.

WRITING CENTER: Students worked either with a partner or individually to write and illustrate recipes or creative animal stories. Recipes included pizza, pancakes, and ice cream. Titles of the student stories included "The Spotted Giraffe," "The Funny Duck," and "The Wolf Comes to School." The completed stories were placed in our classroom library so that other students could read them. The students read the stories to small groups during Stage 3 of our lesson.

LITERATURE CIRCLES: I provided each group with a Semantic Map blackline on which I had written the focus word and the categories. The groups completed their maps, made connections to their books, read and discussed the books, and added information to the map as necessary.

(STAGE 3) Teacher-Facilitated Whole-Group Reflection

SHARE: Students met in small groups to share and discuss their completed Semantic Maps from Stage 2 and their work from the centers and literature circles. The students also shared their student-authored recipes and books with their small groups. Then each group shared examples of its applications with the whole class.

REFLECT: We talked about why we need to know about words and how using graphic organizers such as the Semantic Map helps us to focus on words we will be reading. Jared said, "This is good because we get to think about the word before we read it in a book." The students agreed. Angela said, "I like that it has all the ovals. What is in them is all different and when I want to remember things about the word, I picture what's in the ovals."

SET NEW GOALS: The students decided that they were comfortable using the Semantic Map with narrative (story) text, but they wanted to learn to use it with informational text. That became our new goal.

Assessment Options

I observed students throughout the lesson and used the completed Semantic Maps and students' self-assessment to assess their understanding and application of this technique. I used whisper-reading to informally assess fluency and completed running records with selected students. I also commented on the student-authored books and recipes, paying close attention to how they used the vocabulary of the story in their writing.

LESSON 2 Concept of Definition Maps

STAGE 1 Teacher-Directed Whole-Group Instruction

TEXT: *The Very Hungry Caterpillar* (Carle, 1981)

EXPLAIN: I explained the comprehension strategy knowing how words work and focused on the Concept of Definition Map. I said, "We use Concept of Definition Maps to make connections between words and ideas we already know and information we discover in texts." I also noted that we could record what we already know about the topic on the Concept of Definition Map before reading; after reading, if needed, we could add more information we had learned from our reading. Next, I said, "When we finish our Concept of Definition Maps, we will use them to write summaries." Then I explained that Concept of Definition Maps were different from Semantic Maps because Concept Maps ask us for specific information: what the focus word is, what a good comparison would be, how we would describe the focus word, and what three examples would be.

DEMONSTRATE: I demonstrated by using a think-aloud, a posterboard, and a read-aloud of *The Very Hungry Caterpillar*. I began by introducing the Concept of Definition Map blackline, which I had enlarged and placed on the board the previous day (see Appendix F, p. 207). I wrote *caterpillar*, the topic for our Concept of Definition Map, in the center oval marked "focus word," and I said, "Everything we write on our Concept of Definition Map is going to be about

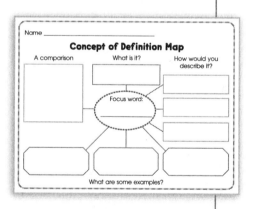

caterpillars." I moved my hand around the map and stopped to talk about each category of information. As I was pointing, I said, "The first thing we need to know is what a caterpillar is. Next, we will need to describe the caterpillar. Then we will need to tell three things that caterpillars do. (I had adapted the question for the last category.) Next, I read aloud the first category of information, "What is it?" I thought aloud and said, "I know a caterpillar is an insect." Then I wrote *insect* in the space provided on the posterboard. I continued my demonstration by examining the section labeled "How would you describe it?" and thinking aloud about what I see when I visualize a caterpillar. I said, "I am going to close my eyes and create a picture in my mind of a caterpillar. Why don't you close your eyes and create a picture in your mind of a caterpillar?" Then I said, "I see a small insect." Kyra said, "I see a fuzzy insect," and Alyssa said, "I see a slow insect." Then I wrote the three descriptions in the boxes provided: "small, fuzzy, slow." We stopped briefly to quickly sketch the pictures we had created in our minds and share them with partners. Then I asked the students what we knew about caterpillars so far, and as I pointed to the completed sections of the Concept Map, I said, "A caterpillar is an insect that is small, fuzzy, and slow." As I said it, I wrote it on the part of the board I had labeled "Concept of Definition Map Summary."

GUIDE: Next, I prompted the students to work with partners to complete the remaining section of the map: three things a caterpillar does. The pairs shared their ideas and the students suggested writing "eats, crawls, turns into a butterfly" in the spaces provided on the map. (See Figure 5-3 for our completed Concept of Definition Map.) Then I added that information to our Concept Map Summary and the students and I read it together. It said:

A caterpillar is a bug that is small, fuzzy, and slow.
It eats, crawls, and turns into a butterfly.

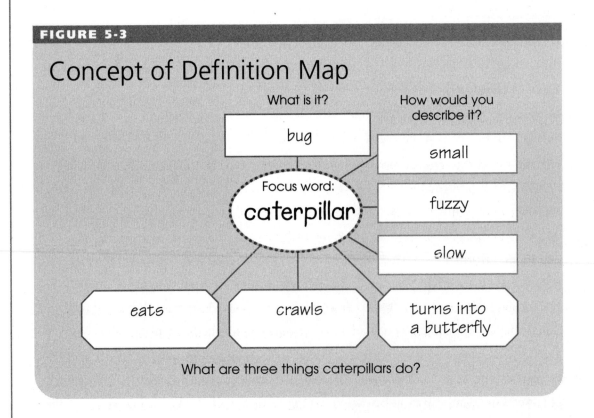

FIGURE 5-3

Concept of Definition Map

PRACTICE: I introduced Eric Carle's book *The Very Hungry Caterpillar* to the students. I showed the cover, read the title, and said, "I wonder why the caterpillar is hungry." The students offered some suggestions, including that the caterpillar couldn't find any food and because caterpillars are so slow that other insects get to the food first. Next, I said, "I wonder if the very hungry caterpillar will get some food to eat in the story." Then I read the story aloud to the class and we talked about what the very hungry caterpillar ate. Finally, we revisited our Concept of Definition Map summary and read it together. Then we talked about what connections we could make from our Concept Map to our book. These included that caterpillars are fuzzy and they turn into butterflies.

REFLECT: We reflected on how we used the Concept of Definition Map to help us understand what we read. We also talked about how the Concept Map Summary helped us to put our ideas together. Finally, we talked about how we could use the maps with other texts in other settings. The students were very excited about learning how to use Concept of Definition Maps and summaries. Edward said, "There is a lot about caterpillars in our Concept Map and putting it in a summary makes it easy to remember."

STAGE 2 Teacher-Guided Small-Group Instruction

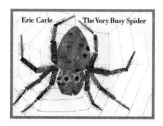

TEXT: *The Very Busy Spider* (Carle, 1989)
(Texts varied according to students' abilities.)

REVIEW: I reminded the students about the comprehension strategies good readers use and focused on knowing how words work and using Concept of Definition Maps.

GUIDE: I gave the small group of students Concept of Definition Map blacklines and explained that our focus word would be *spider*. The students wrote *spider* in the space for the focus word on the Concept of Definition Map blacklines. We briefly discussed some things we knew about spiders and then I guided the students to work with a partner to provide information about spiders for the first category on their Concept of Definition Map. Some students wrote *bug* and others wrote *insect*. I continued to guide the students as they completed the maps. The next information required on the map was to describe a spider. I asked the students to close their eyes and picture a spider before they wrote their descriptive words or phrases. Students' recorded responses included "tiny," "fast," and "lots of legs." We discussed each pair's responses, and I asked, "What do we know about spiders so far?" Then, using the summary frame we had used in Stage 1, we read together,

"A spider is an insect that is tiny, fast, and has lots of legs." Next, we discussed three things that a spider does. Students' responses included "crawls," "spins webs," and "catches flies." When the students had completed their maps, we summarized what we had written. We said, "A spider is a bug that is tiny, fast, and has lots of legs. A spider crawls, spins webs, and catches flies." Next, I introduced *The Very Busy Spider*. I showed the cover of the book and said, "The title of this book is *The Very Busy Spider* and it was written by Eric Carle. What other books do we know that Eric Carle wrote?" Because Eric Carle is one of our favorite authors, each of the students responded with a different title. Then I asked why they thought the spider in the story was busy. There were a number of logical responses, including that he was spinning a web. Next, the students read the first half of the book and we discussed what they read. For example, Greg said, "The story is about a spider spinning a web." Jeanine said, "And the thread is coming out of the spider's body. I didn't know the thread came out of the spider's body." Kirsten said, "It's not thread to use to sew. It is silky thread." Jameel said, "The spider meets a cow and horse and sheep. They want her to do things, but she keeps making her web."

PRACTICE: Students practiced by continuing to read to the end of the text. After we discussed what they had read, we revisited the Concept of Definition Maps we had completed before reading. I asked the students if anything on our map was confirmed in the story, and they pointed out that the spider in the story was busy spinning a web to catch a fly, just as our map said. Then we read our Concept Map Summary again. Our completed Concept of Definition Map is featured in Figure 5-4.

REREAD, RETELL, AND REFLECT: In the second reading, pairs of students whisper-read and I checked for fluency by listening to each student as he or she read a few pages. Next, we orally retold the story and reflected on how making a Concept of Definition Map helped us learn about spiders and make connections between what we knew and what we read. Timothy said, "Before today, when I thought about spiders, I just knew that they could bite." James said, "I like the way the little summary puts everything together." Lila said, "The pictures in the book helped me to understand how a spider spins a web. We have spiders in our yard, but I have only seen webs when they are finished." Finally, we discussed how we could use Concept of Definition Maps and Concept Map Summaries to help us understand words in other texts.

FIGURE 5-4

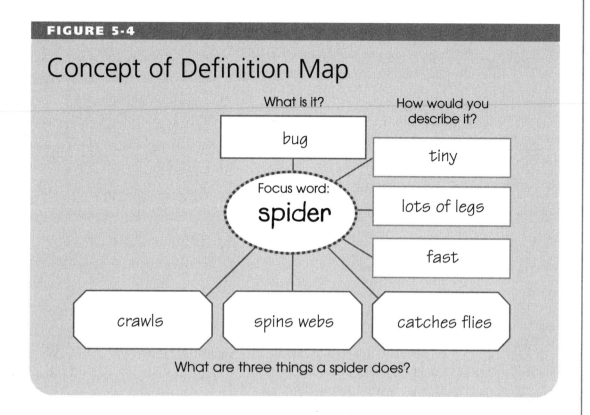

Concept of Definition Map

What is it?

How would you describe it?

bug

Focus word:
spider

tiny

lots of legs

fast

crawls

spins webs

catches flies

What are three things a spider does?

Student-Facilitated Centers

DRAMA CENTER: Students used finger puppets to incorporate the language of the stories to retell them. Puppets from students' favorite Eric Carle stories were available, including a caterpillar, a butterfly, a spider, a cricket, a ladybug, and assorted other props.

MAKING AND WRITING WORDS CENTER: Students practiced a combination of Making Words and Making and Writing Words, using mystery words that were insect names, such as *spider* and *butterfly*. The students used magnetic letters to spell the words and then wrote them in their journals.

WRITING CENTER: Pairs of students used their completed Concept Map Summaries to write and illustrate poems or stories about insects they had learned about. Some of the students used poem or story frames; others did not. Titles of their poems and stories included "The Wiggly Worm," "Spiderman's Spider Web," and "The Pretty Butterfly." When they finished writing, the partners read to each other what they had written. In Stage 3, they read their work to a small group.

Student-Facilitated Routines

LITERATURE CIRCLES: Students completed Concept of Definition Maps and summaries as they read stories and informational books about insects we know. Students used Concept of Definition blacklines I had prepared for the books they were reading. I printed the focus words on the forms and the students completed them. They worked with partners to record initial information, read the books, and complete the maps. They shared their map information and summaries during group discussion.

CROSS-AGE READING EXPERIENCES: Students completed Concept of Definition Maps with a partner while listening to books on tape or trio reading about different types of insects with a peer and a cross-age partner. After revisiting and revising their maps, the students worked together to write Concept of Definition Map summaries.

(STAGE 3)   Teacher-Facilitated Whole-Group Reflection

SHARE: Students shared their Concept of Definition Maps and summaries from Stage 2 in small groups. Then we discussed selected examples as a whole class.

REFLECT: We reflected on how knowing how words work and using Concept of Definition Maps helped us to understand what we read. We also talked about how well we could use the maps and that even though we had used them with narrative (story) text, we could also use them with informational texts.

SET NEW GOALS: We decided to continue working on knowing how words work by learning about Vocabulary Bookmark Technique.

Assessment Options

I used observation, students' completed Concept of Definition Maps and summaries, discussion, and students' self-assessments during this lesson. The assessments were a natural part of each stage of the lesson.

LESSON 3 Synonym Rhymes

STAGE 1 Teacher-Directed Whole-Group Instruction

EXPLAIN: I explained to the students that we were going to learn more about how words work by engaging in Synonym Rhymes (see Appendix F, p. 210), a fun technique in which we use nursery rhymes or poems we know and change them by using synonyms, words that have similar meanings. I said, "You will know the nursery rhymes that we will use, but we will change a few of the words. We will focus on using words that have the same meanings. We will be able to use our thesauruses to help us if we need them."

DEMONSTRATE: I used an overhead projector and a think-aloud to demonstrate. I had placed the rhyme "Jack and Jill" on a transparency on the overhead. I read it to the students and told them I was going to use this very familiar rhyme as a way to learn synonyms. The first transparency read:

> Jack and Jill went up the hill
>
> To fetch a pail of water.
>
> Jack fell down and broke his crown,
>
> And Jill came tumbling after.

Then I showed the students the second transparency, which contained the rhyme with one word deleted from each line:

> Jack and Jill _____ up the hill
>
> To _____ a pail of water.
>
> Jack fell down and broke his _____,
>
> And Jill came _____ after.

I said, "I am going to complete the rhyme using synonyms of the words that have been left out." I read "Jack and Jill _____ up the hill" and thought aloud, "I need a synonym, or word that means nearly the same as *went*. I'm going to close my eyes and visualize Jack

---

Name_____

Synonym Rhymes

Part One: Replace each missing word with a synonym.

Jack and Jill _____ up the hill

To _____ a pail of water.

Jack fell down and broke his _____

And Jill came _____ after.

Part Two: Write a silly version of a rhyme using the same structure.

_____

_____

_____

_____

and Jill going up a hill. They are going up a hill, so instead of *went*, I will say Jack and Jill *climbed* up a hill." Then I asked the students to work with a partner and try to think of other synonyms for *went*. They were able to use their student thesauruses, which I reminded them were formatted just like their student dictionaries. Their suggestions included "walked up a hill" and "ran up a hill." We discussed our options and decided to use *climb* in our rhyme. I used similar reasoning to replace the word *fetch* with a synonym. I said, "I know that *to fetch* means to get something because dogs fetch balls when we throw them. So, I'm thinking of saying Jack and Jill climbed up the hill to *get* a pail of water. But before I decide, I'm going to check my thesaurus." When I looked in the thesaurus, I found that *obtain* was a synonym for *get*. We discussed the possibilities and we decided to add *obtain* to our synonym rhyme. I repeated our version of the rhyme so far. I said, "Jack and Jill climbed up a hill to obtain a pail of water."

GUIDE: I prompted the students to continue working with their partners. I said, "Jack fell down and broke his crown. What synonym or word that has a similar meaning can you think of for *crown*?" As they discussed, I monitored by walking around the class, listening to what they were saying, and noticing that, in this case, most pairs were using their student thesauruses. When it seemed that they were ready to respond, I asked the pairs what synonyms they would suggest. Their ideas included *head*, *skull*, and *cranium*. We decided to add *cranium* to our synonym rhyme.

PRACTICE: We practiced by finding synonyms for *tumbling*. Students worked with their partners and each pair found a viable synonym. Their suggestions included *falling*, *somersaulting*, and *stumbling*. We decided to add *somersaulting* to our rhyme. Then we read our synonym rhyme together:

> Jack and Jill <u>climbed</u> up a hill
>
> To <u>obtain</u> a pail of water.
>
> Jack fell <u>down</u> and broke his <u>cranium</u>
>
> And Jill came <u>somersaulting</u> after.

REFLECT: We reflected on how using existing rhymes helps us know more about how words work because we can replace certain words with different words that mean nearly the same. Students said it was fun to use rhymes they knew and change them by using synonyms. They also enjoyed having another opportunity to use their student thesauruses. They continue to be amazed that so many words have synonyms. They also commented on how easy it was to create a Synonym Rhyme once they had worked with the pattern. They said next time they wanted to try creating transformations that kept the rhyming pattern of the original rhyme. I asked them what they could use to help them think of good rhyming words and they suggested the rhyming dictionary that we have in the classroom. I told them I would put that at the Writing Center so they could use it as a resource in Stage 2.

STAGE 2 Teacher-Guided Small-Group Instruction

REVIEW: I reviewed the comprehension strategies good readers use and then focused on knowing how words work and using Synonym Rhymes to learn new words. I introduced the rhyme "Mary Had a Little Lamb" and told the students that we were going to turn it into a Synonym Rhyme. The original rhyme goes like this:

Mary had a little lamb, its fleece was white as snow.

And everywhere that Mary went, the lamb was sure to go.

GUIDE: I shared the following version of the rhyme, which had three words missing:

Mary had a _____ lamb,

Its fleece was white as snow.

And everywhere that Mary_____,

The lamb was _____ to go.

Next, I guided the students to find synonyms for the words that had been removed. I reminded them that they could use our student thesauruses as resources if they needed them. They started with *little* and offered several suggestions including *small*, *tiny*, and *petite*. They decided to use *tiny* and recorded that in the first blank. Next, they looked for a synonym for *went*. They suggested *walked* and *traveled* and decided to add *traveled* to the synonym rhyme. They read the rhyme and thought that their choices "sounded good."

PRACTICE: They practiced by finding a synonym for *sure*, the last blank in the rhyme. They suggested *certain* and added it to the synonym rhyme. Here is their final version of the rhyme:

> Mary had a <u>tiny</u> lamb,
>
> Its fleece was white as snow.
>
> And everywhere that Mary <u>traveled</u>,
>
> The lamb was <u>certain</u> to go.

REFLECT: We reflected on how much fun wordplay is and how we can use our thesauruses to help us learn new words. The students said they really liked writing Synonym Rhymes and were looking forward to doing some others.

Student-Facilitated Centers

ART CENTER: Students used crayons and markers to illustrate their Synonym Rhymes. Then they displayed them in our class gallery.

ART CENTER: Students illustrated their favorite nursery rhymes and poems and shared their work with others at the center. In Stage 3, they shared their illustrations in small groups and then hung them in our class gallery.

WRITING CENTER: I placed numerous poems at this center. I typed the original poem on the left side of the page and the version of the poem with deleted words on the right side of the page. The students worked alone or with a partner and chose one or more poems to rewrite as Synonym Poems.

(STAGE 3) Teacher-Facilitated Whole-Group Reflection

SHARE: Students shared the Synonym Rhymes they had created in Stage 2. They were very excited about these rhymes, especially the silly ones.

REFLECT: We discussed the importance of learning synonyms and using them effectively in our speaking, reading, and writing. We also reflected on how important good resources such as student thesauruses can be, especially when writing. Finally, we talked about how synonyms help us to use different words to communicate our ideas.

SET NEW GOALS: The students felt comfortable with writing Synonym Rhymes, so we decided our new goal would be to learn to write Antonym Rhymes and Poems.

Assessment Options

I used observation and the completed Synonym Rhymes to assess students during this lesson. I gathered a lot of information about their writing and their ability to use student thesauruses as I watched them work on their rhymes during Stage 2.

LESSON 4 Semantic Question Maps

STAGE 1 Teacher-Directed Whole-Group Instruction

TEXT: *Nature's Green Umbrella* (Gibbons, 1997)

EXPLAIN: I began by explaining how words work and reminding students about the graphophonic, syntactic, and semantic cueing systems (see Chapter 3, Phonics). I emphasized that the word *semantic* relates to meaning. Then I focused on Semantic Question Maps (see Appendix F, p. 209) and how they can help us to learn about the meanings of words. I pointed out that the Semantic Question Map asks us specific questions about the focus word that would help direct our thinking.

DEMONSTRATE: I demonstrated by using a read-aloud, a think-aloud, and a poster-size Semantic Question Map. I introduced the text by reading the title and explaining that it was an informational text that would give us facts about rain forests. Next, I shared the Semantic Question Map I had drawn on the posterboard before class. There was a center oval for the focus word, and webbed question categories emerged from it, including "Where are the rain forests?" "What lives in the rain forest?" "What comes from the rain forest?" and "What can we do to save the rain forest?" I said, "I will write *rain forest* inside the oval because that is the focus word for our map." Then I said, "Now I need to think about what I already know about the rain forest." I read the first category, "Where are the rain forests?" And I said, "I think there is a rain forest in South America, so I will write 'South

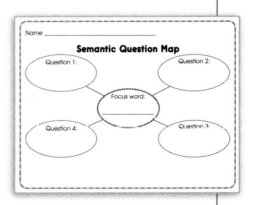

America' underneath this category." Then I thought aloud about what I knew about each of the remaining categories and wrote an answer under each one: "animals," "wood," "write letters." I explained to the students that I would read information about the rain forest and revisit the Semantic Question Map to verify or revise the ideas I had written on the map. I explained that I could also include additional information we might learn from the text. Then I read aloud the first three pages of *Nature's Green Umbrella*. When I finished, I returned to the Semantic Question Map and noted that the information I had included in the map was verified by the text. Next, I reviewed each category to see if I had learned any new information that I could add to the map. The students also contributed suggestions based on my reading of the text.

GUIDE: I guided pairs of students to think about the categories of our Semantic Question Map as they listened to me read another section of *Nature's Green Umbrella*. The text provided more information to add to our map, so when I asked the students what they would like to add to our Semantic Question Map, they suggested ideas such as "oxygen," "the Amazon," and "birds and bugs." I recorded the students' ideas on our map in response to the appropriate question.

PRACTICE: Students practiced by listing additional details to add to our Semantic Question Map as I read another section of text. When I finished, they added "rain," "food," and "medicine" to our map and noted that some of the information we had previously written on our map was verified by the text. I read aloud the last section of the text and the students wrote additional details to add to our Semantic Question Map. When I finished the last section of text, the students added "use select cutting," "limiting what can be taken," and "North America, Australia, Africa, and Asia" to our map and again noted that some of the information we had previously written on our map had been verified by the ideas in this text. We used our completed Semantic Question Map to create an oral summary. Our completed Semantic Question Map appears in Figure 5-5.

REFLECT: We reflected on what we had learned about the rain forest and on how the Semantic Question Map helped us to organize our thinking. We decided that we would leave our map on display and add new information to the categories as we learned more about the rain forest. The students asked if we could create other Semantic Question Maps for the layers of the rain forest and I noted that we would be doing that in Stage 2. We also talked about how the organization of the map helped us to remember the information. Finally, we discussed how we would use Semantic Question Maps with other texts in other settings.

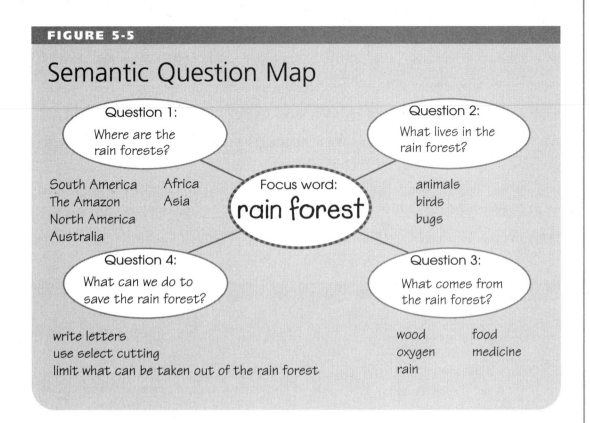

FIGURE 5-5

Semantic Question Map

Question 1:
Where are the rain forests?

South America   Africa
The Amazon   Asia
North America
Australia

Focus word:
rain forest

Question 2:
What lives in the rain forest?

animals
birds
bugs

Question 4:
What can we do to save the rain forest?

write letters
use select cutting
limit what can be taken out of the rain forest

Question 3:
What comes from the rain forest?

wood   food
oxygen   medicine
rain

STAGE 2   Teacher-Guided Small-Group Instruction

TEXT: *Save the Rain Forests* (Fowler, 1997)
(Texts varied according to students' abilities.)

REVIEW: I began by reviewing the comprehension strategies that good readers use and focused on knowing how words work and Semantic Question Maps. I introduced *Save the Rain Forests* and explained that this book contains factual information about the rain forest. I shared the cover and title and read aloud the first three pages. We discussed the reading and then began working on a Semantic Question Map that focused on rain forests. This time the questions were "What plants live in the rain forest?" and "What animals live in the rain forest?" I guided the students in reading the next five pages of the text, prompting as necessary. They paused when they had finished reading, and we discussed the information and made additions to our Semantic Question Map. The students added "ferns, mosses, orchids, and vines" to the map in response to "What plants are in the rain forest?"

PRACTICE: Students practiced by continuing to read the text. When they had finished, they added "deer and tapir" and "capybaras, orangutan, jaguar, and bats" to the map in response to "What animals live in the rain forest?"

READ, RETELL, AND REFLECT: Rather than reread this text, students suggested that we check texts we had already read for more information about the rain forest. Students began to reread segments of *Nature's Green Umbrella* by Gail Gibbons and other theme-related texts, so they could add information to the map we had been working on in small groups. Our Semantic Question Map about the rain forest, as it appeared at the end of our guided small-group lesson, appears in Figure 5-6.

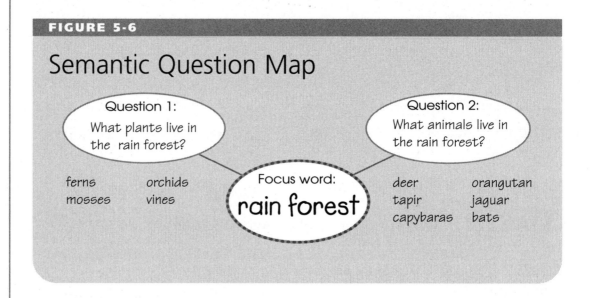

FIGURE 5-6

Semantic Question Map

Question 1:
What plants live in the rain forest?

ferns   orchids
mosses   vines

Focus word:
rain forest

Question 2:
What animals live in the rain forest?

deer   orangutan
tapir   jaguar
capybaras bats

Student-Facilitated Centers

ABC CENTER: Students worked in pairs on the computer to create a page for our class rain forest alphabet book. They had learned many new vocabulary words while studying the rain forest, so creating a class rain forest book helped them to focus on what they had learned. When this project was complete, we shared the alphabet book in class, exhibited it during our theme celebration, and placed it in our classroom library.

POETRY CENTER: Students used Semantic Question Maps they had previously completed to write and illustrate acrostic poems about the rain forest.

THEME CENTER: Students self-selected texts from the Rain Forest Animals Series written by Helen Frost and published by Pebble Books that I had placed in the theme center. They worked either individually or with a partner to complete a Semantic Question Map.

WRITING CENTER: Students used a Semantic Question Map they had completed previously to write and illustrate a brochure about a layer of the rain forest.

Student-Facilitated Routines

CROSS-AGE READING EXPERIENCES: Students read with a peer and a cross-age partner. They began completing the Semantic Question Map prior to reading and added information as necessary during and after reading. Then they used the completed map to create an oral summary.

LITERATURE CIRCLES: Students used the Semantic Question Map to take notes as they read the text the group had selected. After reading the text and completing the maps, students used them to facilitate discussion.

(STAGE 3) Teacher-Facilitated Whole-Group Reflection

SHARE: Students shared their completed Semantic Question Maps from Stage 2 in small groups. Then they shared selected maps, poems, paragraphs, and stories with the whole group.

REFLECT: We reflected on how completing Semantic Question Maps helped to guide our reading and on how well we could use them. Bryan said, "The Semantic Question Map helped me to pay close attention as we were reading. I had to focus on finding out information to answer our questions." The students seemed to take great pride in their completed Semantic Question Maps.

SET NEW GOALS: We all felt comfortable using the Semantic Question Map. The students were especially pleased that the completed maps could be used as the basis of discussion and writing. We decided to extend our goal of knowing how words work by learning how to use the Vocabulary Bookmarks Technique.

Assessment Options

I used a variety of assessments, including observation, running records, students' strategy applications, student writing, and student self-assessments during this lesson.

LESSON 5   Vocabulary Bookmark Technique

STAGE 1   Teacher-Directed Whole-Group Instruction

TEXT: *Whales* (Gibbons, 1991)

EXPLAIN: I explained to the students that we would be focusing on a new way to learn vocabulary called Vocabulary Bookmarks (see Appendix F, p. 211). I said, "Vocabulary Bookmarks will probably become your favorite way to learn words, because you get to choose the words you want to learn. While we're reading, you will select a word you want the whole class to discuss. It can be a word we know that we want others to know or a word we don't know at all." I explained that when we had decided which word we wanted to use, we would write it on a Vocabulary Bookmark. We would also write what we thought the word meant and the page on which it was found. I explained that it was important to include the page and paragraph so that we could go back and read how the word was used. I said, "After our bookmarks are completed, we will discuss the words as a class, so we can better understand the meaning of the word, how it was used in the text, and how we can use it in our reading, writing, and conversations."

DEMONSTRATE: To demonstrate, I introduced Gail Gibbons's book *Whales* to the class and read the first four pages aloud. As I was reading, I paused at the word *ancestors* on page 4. (*Whales* does not have page numbers, so, before class, a few upper-grade volunteers and I inserted them in pencil in each copy of the book.) I knew this would be a word that the students might not understand. I wrote the word on an enlarged template of a Vocabulary Bookmark. I thought aloud as I wrote what I thought *ancestors* meant. I said, "I can see how *ancestors* is used in the text. On page 4, the book says that the 'first ancestors of whales lived more than 50 million years ago.' I think *ancestors* means whoever came before. For us, examples of our ancestors would be our parents, grandparents, and great-grandparents." I wrote on the Vocabulary Bookmark what I thought *ancestors* meant, and I also wrote the page number (4) and the paragraph number (1). We went back to page 4 and read together the line that contained *ancestors*. As we finished reading the page, the students and I discussed the idea I had written on the Vocabulary Bookmark and what I read from the text. The students thought that ancestors were those that came before.

Jeremy said, "So, if our ancestors are our parents and grandparents, whales' ancestors must be whales that lived before whales now—like today's whales' parents and grandparents all the way back to a long time ago." We decided that what I had written on the Vocabulary Bookmark was very close to what the book said the word meant. I explained that when we use Vocabulary Bookmarks, we should always verify what we think the word means with how it is used in the text, and, if needed, with a dictionary.

GUIDE: To guide the students, I continued to read aloud. The students worked in partners and had their own books, so they could follow along. I had distributed copies of the Vocabulary Bookmark blackline for them to use. After I read five more pages, I asked the students to choose a word they thought the class should discuss and write it on a Vocabulary Bookmark. Some of the words that the pairs chose were *flukes, balance,* and *blowholes.* The students discussed their word, found it in the text, and then wrote what they thought the word meant on the Vocabulary Bookmark. They also recorded the page and paragraph numbers. Then they discussed their words. For example, Kenny and Beth had chosen *fluke* as their word. They told us it was on page 7 in paragraph 1. We turned to that page, and Beth said, "The book says that the whales' tails are called flukes, so we think that's what they are. We know the book tells what flukes are, but we wanted to learn this word so we would always know it." We also discussed *balance* and *blowhole.* Annette and Robbie read that section about balance and explained what they thought *balance* (page 7, paragraph 1) meant by making connections to balance beams they had learned about while watching the Olympics. When they checked with the dictionary, their ideas were very close to the word's meaning. Several pairs chose the word *blowhole,* which was on page 8 in paragraph 1. When Alex and Teresa read that section, they decided that the whales' blowholes were like our noses. The dictionary verified that they were correct. Then we discussed all three words and how much knowing what they meant helped us to understand more about whales. Pairs of students practiced talking about whales, using the words from the Vocabulary Bookmarks.

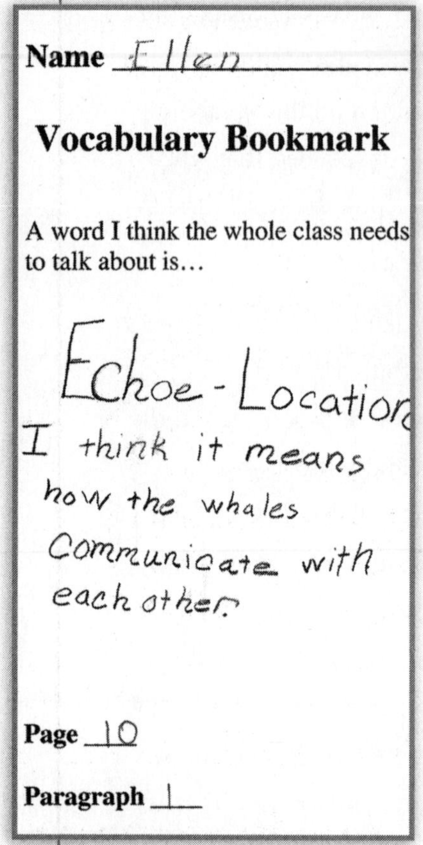

Name _Ellen_

Vocabulary Bookmark

A word I think the whole class needs to talk about is...

Echoe - Location
I think it means
how the whales
Communicate with
each other.

Page _10_

Paragraph _1_

FIGURE 5-7

PRACTICE: To practice, I read aloud to the end of the first section of the book. As I read, the students wrote on their Vocabulary Bookmarks other words that they wanted the whole class to discuss. I reminded them that they needed to write down the page and the paragraph, so that we could go back and find the words. Some of the words that the students wrote on their Vocabulary Bookmarks were *echolocation*, *pods*, and *migration*. Students wrote what they thought the words meant and the pages and paragraphs where we could find them. Students discussed their words and their meanings at their tables. I went to each group and listened to their discussions of their words. Then we shared the words with the whole class. Figure 5-7 shows Ellen's "echolocation" Vocabulary Bookmark.

REFLECT: To reflect, we discussed that it was helpful to talk about one another's words because it helped us learn more words. David said, "Sometimes I think I know what a word means, but when we talk about them I learn more about the words." Janeece said, "I like choosing our own words and how the book helps us know what they mean."

I said, "When we can figure out a word's meaning from the text, it's called using context clues. We use the information around a word to help us figure out what the word means."

(STAGE 2) Teacher-Guided Small-Group Instruction

TEXT: *Wolves* (Simon, 1993)
(Texts varied according to students' abilities.)

REVIEW: To review, I reminded students about the Vocabulary Bookmark Technique and how context clues help us figure out what words mean. I suggested the students choose a word that was unfamiliar to them or a word they wanted to know more about.

GUIDE: To guide the students, I read them the first page of *Wolves*, by Seymour Simon. As I read, I chose the word *eerie* to write on my Vocabulary Bookmark. We then reread the sentence aloud to see how *eerie* was used. The line read, "Suddenly the quiet is broken by the eerie howling of a wolf." Sasha, one of my students, thought it meant spooky. Kelly thought it meant creepy. Many of the other students agreed. Next, I chose the word *savage* to discuss. Mandy thought *savage* meant wild or mean. Nora thought it meant dangerous. The line in the text read, "Are wolves savage and destructive hunters of people and livestock?" Finally, I reminded the students that they should look for words they wanted to discuss as a group as they read the rest of the text.

PRACTICE: Students read the rest of the text while looking for words they wanted to discuss as a group. I gave students in the small group two Vocabulary Bookmarks apiece, so they could write their word choices, page numbers, and paragraphs. Some of the words the students chose to talk about were *cowardly*, *domesticated*, *tundra*, *interbreeding*, and *dominance*. We discussed their words as a group, focusing on meaning, parts of speech and how we could use them in our conversations and our writing. Erika's completed bookmark appears in Figure 5-8.

Students also put some of the words in personal vocabulary sketching dictionaries that they had made. (These were 15 pieces of paper stapled together with a sheet of construction paper for a cover.) A letter of the alphabet was written at the top of each sheet. The students wrote their words and their meanings in these dictionaries. The students enjoyed drawing a picture and writing a sentence to help them remember the meaning of a word.

REFLECT: We reflected on how we can use Vocabulary Bookmark Technique to help one another learn many new words and their meanings. The students said they enjoyed being able to choose their words and share their ideas about the words.

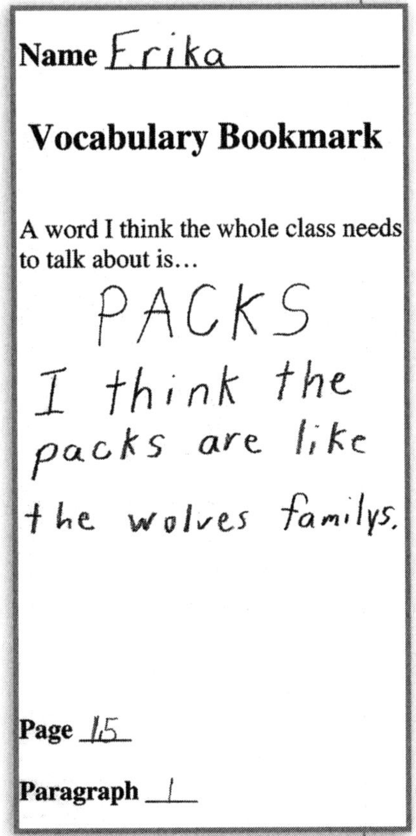

FIGURE 5-8

> **Name** Erika
>
> **Vocabulary Bookmark**
>
> A word I think the whole class needs to talk about is...
>
> PACKS
> I think the packs are like the wolves familys.
>
> **Page** 15
>
> **Paragraph** 1

Student-Facilitated Centers

THEME CENTER: I placed four different animal books at this center. The students worked in small groups, chose a book to read, completed two Vocabulary Bookmarks, verified their definitions in dictionaries, and discussed them as a group. During Stage 3, I asked the students to get into four groups, depending on which book they had read. They brought their Vocabulary Bookmarks to the group to share. Students discussed their words and meanings as I moved around the room and listened to each group.

WRITING CENTER: The students brought completed Vocabulary Bookmarks to this center and wrote their new words into their personal vocabulary sketching dictionaries. They wrote the word and what it meant. Then they drew a picture and wrote a sentence.

(STAGE 3) Teacher-Facilitated Whole-Group Reflection

SHARE: Students shared their Vocabulary Bookmarks and their entries from their personal vocabulary sketching dictionaries in small groups.

REFLECT: Students commented that they liked Vocabulary Bookmark Technique because everyone could learn about the words they selected. Many also felt that discussing the words helped them to better comprehend the text.

SET NEW GOALS: We decided to keep working on increasing our vocabularies by learning to use Vocabulary Bookmark Technique with stories.

Assessment Options

I used a variety of assessments, including observation. I was especially interested in observing the words students chose. I also used students' completed Vocabulary Bookmarks, student writing, and student self-assessments during this lesson.

Final Thoughts on This Chapter

The lessons in this chapter integrated research findings and current beliefs about best practice in teaching vocabulary. The research-based Guided Comprehension Model for the Primary Grades provided a format that integrated direct and guided instruction as well as numerous opportunities for independent practice. Texts at a variety of levels and various modes of reader response were incorporated to accommodate students' abilities. Reflection and informal assessments permeated the lessons, which were designed to foster students' understanding and use of vocabulary.

It's important to note that although the lessons featured in this chapter were taught at particular grade levels, they can be adapted to accommodate other levels and needs. For example, these lessons were taught by first- (Lessons 1 and 2), second- (Lesson 3), and third-grade teachers (Lessons 4 and 5), but they are easily adaptable to teach upper-grade students who need to learn how to acquire vocabulary. Students develop at their own rates, and their needs for different skills and strategies vary. Ideas to adapt the lessons to accommodate English language learners, struggling readers, and special needs students include adding more modeling and demonstration, changing texts, providing more examples or focusing on fewer examples, providing time for more guided instruction or independent practice, and changing the level of word choice or questioning. Most of the lessons address skills and strategies that develop over time and continue to need reinforcement.

In the next chapter, we examine the role of the other Guided Comprehension strategies in the reading process. We begin by addressing theoretical underpinnings of comprehension and then present a variety of lessons focused on teaching comprehension strategies in the primary grades.

What can we read to learn more about teaching vocabulary?

Blachowicz, C. L., & Fisher, P. (2000). Vocabulary instruction. In M. L. Kamil, P. D. Pearson, & R. Barr (Eds.), *Handbook of reading research* (Vol. 3, pp. 503–523). Mahwah, NJ: Erlbaum.

Buehl, D. (2001). *Classroom strategies for interactive learning* (2nd ed.). Newark, DE: International Reading Association.

International Reading Association. (2002). *IRA Literacy Study Groups vocabulary module.* Newark, DE: International Reading Association.

CHAPTER 6

Comprehension

As reading teachers, our ultimate goal is to help our students construct meaning—to comprehend what they read. To do this, our students need to be active, strategic readers, research tells us. This has resulted in a recent, renewed focus on teaching comprehension strategies (Pearson, 2001) that has particularly impacted reading instruction in the primary grades. In the past, comprehension skills were taught in the primary grades, along with a few comprehension strategies—usually predicting and summarizing— but focusing on teaching a broader range of comprehension strategies in the primary grades is a new development. Recent research indicates that primary-grade students are capable of learning and using a full spectrum of reading comprehension strategies (Hilden & Pressley, 2002; McLaughlin, 2003). Our goal is to teach the strategies so that students can develop a repertoire of strategies they can use as needed.

In Part One of this chapter, we explain what comprehension is, present what the research has to say, and discuss how to integrate the research results in our teaching. In Part Two, we present teacher-authored, classroom-tested Guided Comprehension lessons for teaching reading strategies in the primary grades. The chapter concludes with final thoughts and a short list of suggested readings.

Part One: Research Base

What is comprehension?

Comprehension is the construction of meaning of a written or spoken communication through a reciprocal, holistic interchange of ideas between the interpreter and the message in a particular communicative context. Note: The presumption here is that meaning resides in the intentional problem-solving, thinking processes of the interpreter during such an interchange, that the content of meaning is influenced by that person's prior knowledge and experience, and that the message so constructed by the receiver may or may not be congruent with the message sent (Harris & Hodges, 1995, p. 39).

What does the research tell us?

Reading is a social-constructivist process. Constructivists believe that comprehension takes place when students connect what they know and have experienced to the text they are reading. The more experience learners have with a topic, the easier it is for them to make the connections (Anderson, 1994; Anderson & Pearson, 1984). Cambourne (2002) notes that constructivism has three core assumptions:

- What is learned cannot be separated from the context in which it is learned.

- The reader's purposes or goals are central to what is being learned.

- Knowledge and meaning are socially constructed through the processes of negotiation, evaluation, and transformation.

Research tells us that good readers

- are active and use comprehension strategies to help them derive meaning from text; have goals and constantly monitor the relation between the goals they have set and the text they are reading;

- spontaneously generate questions;

- construct and revise meaning as they read;

- have an awareness of the author's style and purpose;

- read widely (Askew & Fountas, 1998; Duke & Pearson, 2002; Pressley, 2000).

How can we make the research-teaching connection?

The research supports that good readers use comprehension strategies and benefit from print-rich environments and from reading a variety of texts at appropriate levels. In Part Two of this chapter, we present a variety of Guided Comprehension lessons designed to facilitate this process. They are strategy-based; feature direct and guided instructions, as well as opportunities for independent practice in centers and routines; incorporate different genres at a variety of levels; and provide students with plenty of time to read, write, and discuss independently.

Part Two: Lesson Overview

In this chapter, all of the lessons focus on teaching reading comprehension strategies. They specifically address the strategies associated with the Guided Comprehension Model (see Chapter 1). These include the following:

- **PREVIEWING:** a way of introducing the text that includes activating background knowledge, setting a purpose for reading, and predicting (see Lesson 1, Story Impressions).

- **SELF-QUESTIONING:** generating questions to guide thinking while reading (see Lesson 2, "I Wonder" Statements).

- **MAKING CONNECTIONS:** thinking about the text in relationship to self, to texts, and to others (see lesson 3, Drawing Connections).

- **VISUALIZING:** creating mental images while reading (see Lesson 4, Draw and Label Visualizations).

- **KNOWING HOW WORDS WORK:** understanding words through strategic vocabulary development, including the use of the graphophonic, syntactic, and semantic cueing systems to figure out unknown words (see Chapter 3). Readers use all three cueing systems, along with other knowledge of words, to effectively engage with text (see all lessons in Chapter 5).

- **MONITORING:** "Does this make sense?" and clarifying by adapting strategic processes to accommodate the response (see Lesson 5, Bookmark Technique).

- **SUMMARIZING:** extracting essential information, such as the narrative elements (characters, setting, problem, attempts to resolve the problem, and resolution) or the main idea and supporting details from informational text (see Lesson 6, Draw and Label Retelling).

- **EVALUATING:** making judgments while reading (see Lesson 7, Discussion Web).

The lessons that focus on knowing how words work are featured in Chapter 5. The lessons addressing the remaining strategies are presented in this chapter.

Featured texts include *The Grouchy Ladybug* (Carle, 1999); *The Very Lonely Firefly* (Carle, 1999); *Arthur Writes a Story* (Brown, 1996); *Arthur's Reading Race* (Brown, 1996); *Cinder Edna* (Jackson, 1994); *The Three Little Dinosaurs* (Harris, 1999); *Welcome to the Green House* (Yolen, 1993); *The Great Kapok Tree* (Cherry, 1990); *First to Fly* (Busby, 2002); *My Brothers' Flying Machine* (Yolen, 2003); *Duck for President* (Cronin, 2004); *Oh, Ducky* (Slonim, 2003); *The Web Files* (Palatini, 2001); *Mama Played Baseball* (Adler, 2003); *H is for Homerun* (Herzog, 2004); and *Martin's Big Words* (Rappaport, 2001).

The lessons in this chapter are appropriate for all types of learners. In our classrooms we may have students who speak English as a second language, struggling readers, and students with special needs. To accommodate these learners, the lessons include the use of multiple modalities (singing, sketching, and so on), working with partners, books on tape, cross-age experiences, and extra guided instruction for students who struggle. For ideas on further adapting the lessons, see "Final Thoughts" at the end of the chapter.

This section features seven teacher-authored, classroom-tested lessons that each address a specific comprehension strategy. The lessons include teacher think-alouds and student work. They were designed using the Guided Comprehension Model for the Primary Grades (McLaughlin, 2003), which was discussed in Chapter One. Explanations of the comprehension-based teaching ideas and related blacklines can be found in Appendix F (p. 189).

LESSON 1 Story Impressions
Strategy: Previewing

GUIDED COMPREHENSION THEME: Favorite Author Eric Carle

STAGE 1 Teacher-Directed Whole-Group Instruction

TEXT: *The Grouchy Ladybug* (Carle, 1999)

EXPLAIN: I explained to students that when we preview a text we can activate background knowledge, make predictions, and set a purpose for reading. We discussed thinking about what we already know about a topic. I modeled something I already knew about ladybugs by saying, "I know ladybugs can fly." Then I asked students to work with a partner to sketch something they knew about ladybugs. We shared and discussed their drawings. Then I explained that we can use what we know to make predictions or guess what might happen in a story and that one way to do that was by writing a Story Impression. I told the students that writing a Story Impression was like being a detective: We would use clues about the characters, setting, and what happens in a story to write our prediction or what we think might happen in the story.

DEMONSTRATE: I demonstrated by using an overhead projector, a think-aloud, and a Story Impression blackline (see Appendix F, p. 203). I began by introducing a list of words—or clues—to the students. See the graph at right for the words I used.

I reminded the students that these words related to the narrative elements: characters, setting, problem, and solution. I said, "These are the words that answer the questions, Who was in the story? Where did the story take place? What happened in the story? How did the story end?" I reviewed these elements with the students and explained the importance of using each of the words on the list in the order in which

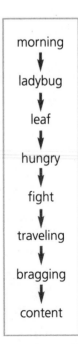

morning
↓
ladybug
↓
leaf
↓
hungry
↓
fight
↓
traveling
↓
bragging
↓
content

it appeared on the list because that is the order in which it appeared in the original story. I pointed out that the arrows connecting the words remind us of the order in which we needed to use them. I shared the title of the book, *The Grouchy Ladybug* (this is optional when using Story Impressions) and reviewed each of the words on the list. Then I reminded the students that after we wrote our story, we would read the original story to check our predictions.

I looked at the first clue on the list—"morning"—and said, "The story must take place in the morning, so I will start the story by writing 'One morning. . .' " Next, I said, "I think the ladybug is the main character in this story, so I will add ladybug to my sentence." Then I finished writing my opening sentence: "One morning a ladybug was sitting near a tree." Then I read the third clue, "leaf," and said, "The ladybug crawled onto a leaf because she was hungry."

GUIDE: I encouraged the students to look at the next clue and think about how the story might continue. I reminded them that we needed to create a problem for the story, and I prompted them with a few questions. I asked them to share their ideas with a partner, and together we came up with a possible problem. I wrote: "The ladybug had to fight other insects for her food."

PRACTICE: The students were excited to take on the role of detectives as we continued writing our story. They worked in small groups to create sentences for the next clue—"traveling." Examples of sentences they created included "The ladybug did not want to fight so she traveled far away" and "After the ladybug ate she went traveling." As we continued, the students developed sentences to complete the Story Impression. The following is an example that shows how Maddy, Kanisha, David, and Michael completed the Story Impression:

> One morning, a ladybug was sitting near a tree. The ladybug crawled onto a leaf because she was hungry. The ladybug had to fight other insects for food. She did not like to fight, so she went traveling to other leaves in search of food because she was really hungry. On the other leaves the ladybug always met other bugs who were bragging that they were better than she was. But then she came to a leaf where there were no other bugs and she was able to eat. Then she was happy and content and fell asleep.

After we shared students' endings to the story, I explained that I would read Eric Carle's *The Grouchy Ladybug* aloud so we could see how he used the clues in his story. When reading the story, I stopped at several points and prompted the students to compare

ways our stories and Eric Carle's were the same and contrast ways our stories and Eric Carle's were different. We used a Comparison/Contrast Chart to record our ideas (see Appendix F, p. 216). When I finished reading *The Grouchy Ladybug*, we discussed the stories and used the original word list to write a class summary of Eric Carle's story.

REFLECT: I prompted the students to reflect on using the Story Impression and on how it helped to prepare us to read the original story. We talked about the importance of previewing before reading a story and how we could use Story Impressions to write predictions about other stories.

STAGE 2   Teacher-Guided Small-Group Instruction

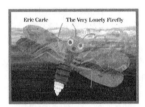

TEXT: *The Very Lonely Firefly* (Carle, 1999)
(Texts varied according to students' abilities.)

REVIEW: I reviewed the comprehension strategies good readers use and then focused on previewing using Story Impressions. I cited a few examples from Stage One and reminded students that we would be detectives and use the clues to write a Story Impression.

GUIDE: I showed the students the title and illustration on the cover of *The Very Lonely Firefly*. We engaged in discussion to activate background knowledge. Students' observations included "Fireflies light up like lights" and "On summer nights I can see fireflies in my yard." Next, I shared a list of clues and reminded students that the clues related to the story elements and needed to be used in the order in which they appeared. The following words were on the list: *sunset, lonely firefly, searching, lightbulb, candle, flashlight, lantern, dog, cat, owl, headlights, fireworks, night, not lonely anymore.* I prompted the students to look at the first few words and start thinking about the story. I explained that Story Impressions were meant to be written by a small group, so they would all be working together to write the story. I reminded them that they needed to introduce a character and setting. The students began their impression by writing, "Once at sunset a lonely firefly was in our yard." Then I guided them to use the next few words to create the problem. The students wrote, "He was searching for something he lost."

PRACTICE: I reminded the students that they needed to use the rest of the words as they finished writing their Story Impression. I guided this process and assisted when invited to do so. When they completed their story, they read it aloud and we discussed their ideas. This is the group's completed Story Impression:

> Once at sunset a lonely firefly was in our yard. He was searching for something he lost. First he used a light bulb to try to help him find it, but that didn't work. Then, he tried a candle, a flashlight, and a lantern, but he still could not find what he lost. Then, he met a dog, a cat, and an owl, and they tried to help him. They saw headlights and fireworks that lit up the sky, but they still could not find what the firefly lost. It was really late at night, so they decided to stop looking for what the firefly lost, and be good friends. Then the lonely firefly was not lonely anymore.

Next, we revisited the illustration and title on the cover of the book and reviewed our predictions. Then the students whisper-read the first three pages of the book. We revisited our predictions, modifying some and making some new ones. The students whisper-read the next section and we continued the process of reading segments and revisiting and revising our predictions as the story progressed. After reading, we compared and contrasted the stories written by the students and by Eric Carle.

REREAD, RETELL, AND REFLECT: Students read the story a second time silently and then we completed an oral retelling. During the silent reading, I asked one student to whisper-read and completed a running record with her. Next, we talked about the Story Impressions we wrote and Eric Carle's story. This led to an interesting discussion of how different authors can write different stories using the same clues. Then we reflected on how previewing helps us to understand what we are reading and how writing Story Impressions help us to make predictions based on what we know. Stephanie noted that "we really need to know a lot about a lot of things when we're reading." This led to a discussion about how much easier it is to read and write when we know something about the topic.

Student-Facilitated Centers and Routine

ART CENTER: Students created Picture Impressions using blacklines containing word lists related to Eric Carle books. They created their Picture Impressions using tissue paper and glue in "Eric Carle–style" collage. The students worked with a partner to select an Eric Carle book and accompanying Picture Impression clues. Then they worked independently to create a picture collage. Next, the partners talked about their Picture Impression and partner-read the original Eric Carle story. As they read, they predicted, verified, and modified their thoughts. Finally, they compared and contrasted their collages with the Eric Carle story.

POETRY CENTER: Students wrote and illustrated Poem Impressions from word lists taken from poems found in *Eric Carle's Animals, Animals*. Students shared their Poem Impressions with a partner and then read the original poem. Next, the partners compared and contrasted their Poem Impressions with the original poem.

THEME CENTER: I placed a variety of Eric Carle books and Story Impression blacklines containing word lists—clues—for a variety of titles at this center. The students worked in groups of four. Each pair wrote a Story Impression and shared it with the other pair. Then the four students read the Eric Carle book and discussed how their stories compared and contrasted with the original story. At the conclusion of the activity, students placed their Story Impressions in their reading portfolios. They would share them with the rest of the class during Stage 3.

LITERATURE CIRCLES: I provided each group with a list of words to create Story Impressions for the theme-related text(s) they were reading. The children worked as a group to create a Story Impression and record it on a large piece of poster paper. When they completed their Story Impression, they partner-read the original Eric Carle book or short story. Then the students gathered in their circle and the discussion leader facilitated the discussion of their Story Impression and the original story.

STAGE 3 | Teacher-Facilitated Whole-Group Reflection

SHARE: Students shared their Story, Picture, and Poem Impressions from Stage 2 in small groups. Then representatives from each group shared with the whole class.

REFLECT: Students reflected on using the various impression techniques and noted that it was fun to use clues to create their own stories, poems, and pictures. They especially enjoyed seeing how their writing and art compared and contrasted to what Eric Carle had created. Their conversation indicated that they enjoyed expressing their ideas through writing, art, and discussion. I especially appreciated the students' perceptions of themselves and Eric Carle as authors and illustrators. We concluded our reflections by noting how previewing—and in this case predicting, in particular—helped us to understand what we read.

SET NEW GOALS: The students' discussions, performances, and self-assessments supported their thoughts that they were quite capable of using Story Impressions to preview text. We decided to extend our goal by learning how to preview informational text.

Assessment Options

I carefully observed the students as they contributed to our whole-class Story Impression and as they created Story Impressions in our guided small groups. I also reviewed the Story Impressions, Comparison–Contrast Charts, and self–assessments they created at the centers and in the Literature Circles.

LESSON 2 "I Wonder" Statements
Strategy: Self-Questioning

GUIDED COMPREHENSION THEME: The Adventures of Arthur the Aardvark

STAGE 1 Teacher-Directed Whole-Group Instruction

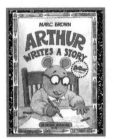

TEXT: *Arthur Writes a Story* (Brown, 1996)

EXPLAIN: I began by explaining Self-Questioning and how "I Wonder" Statements help us self-question as we read. I said, "If we read and wonder, we are always asking questions. Then we read to see if what we wondered actually happened in the text. This helps us to be good, active thinkers and set purposes for our reading."

DEMONSTRATE: I demonstrated "I Wonder" Statements by using a read-aloud, a think-aloud, and an overhead projector. I shared the cover and title of *Arthur Writes a Story* and read aloud the first page. First, I said, "I see Arthur on the cover and his name in the title, so I think this book is about another one of Arthur's adventures." Next, I said, "The title says he is going to write a story. I know that when I write a story I need to focus on what I will be writing about. Mr. Ratburn told Arthur to write about something he knew about, so I wonder if Arthur will write about something he knew about." Then I wrote my "I Wonder" Statement on the transparency of the "I Wonder" Bookmark blackline I had placed on the overhead projector (see Appendix F, p. 204). I read aloud the next three pages to learn if my wonder was verified and create a new "I Wonder" Statement. The section I read included a story Arthur had written entitled "How I Got My Puppy," so I remarked that I had wondered whether Arthur would write about something he knew about and, according to the book, he did. Then I created a new "I Wonder" Statement. I based it on the last page I had read. Arthur had shared his story with D.W., and she had said it was boring and that she thought he should write about elephants. My "I Wonder" Statement, which I recorded on the transparency, was, "I wonder if Arthur will change his story and write about elephants." Then I read the next

---

Name_____

I Wonder Bookmark

Page_____

I wonder _____

_____

_____

because _____

Page_____

I wonder _____

_____

_____

because _____

_____

two pages and said, "I know Arthur changed his story and wrote about elephants because he said there were elephant puppies in his story."

GUIDE: I guided the students' use of "I Wonder" Statements by prompting them to work with a partner to wonder about the section I had just finished reading. Students said they wondered if Arthur was going to change his story again and write about outer space because after Buster told him about that, Arthur was thinking about putting the moon in his story. I recorded their wonder and read aloud the next two pages. They confirmed the students' wonder, and we continued this process with another section of text.

PRACTICE: Next, the students practiced by creating "I Wonder" Statements on their own as I continued to read aloud and stop at designated points. After we shared our wonders, I continued reading aloud so we could learn if our wonders were confirmed, briefly discuss them, and create new ones. When I finished the story, I asked the students to think of an "I Wonder" Statement about the ending. Elaine suggested, "I wonder what will happen the next time Mr. Ratburn asks Arthur to write a story." This prompted a discussion about how writing about what he knew turned out best for Arthur. Carl said, "I think it would be easier to write a story about my dog than about animals and places I don't know." Others agreed and offered examples of topics they had written stories about. These included baseball, pets, and family. I noted that writing a story about Arthur's next adventure was one of the activities students could complete at the Writing Center. Then we revisited the story by watching the video of *Arthur Writes a Story*. Afterward, we discussed how the same story could be shared in a variety of ways, including reading, viewing, and listening.

REFLECT: The students and I reflected by discussing our earlier wonders and how Arthur's topic changed as the story progressed. I was also careful to remind students that when we wonder, we always provide a reason for our thinking. Then we talked about how our "I Wonder" Statements helped us self-question as we read the story and how that encouraged us to think about the text.

(STAGE 2) Teacher-Guided Small-Group Instruction

TEXT: *Arthur's Reading Race* (Brown, 1996)
(Texts varied according to students' abilities.)

REVIEW: I reminded students about the comprehension strategies that good readers use and focused on Self-Questioning using "I Wonder" Statements.

GUIDE: I introduced the text and guided the students' reading of *Arthur's Reading Race*. During my story introduction, I guided the students to use the "I Wonder" Statements before reading to try to predict what would happen, using the cover, title, and a read-aloud of the first few pages for clues. For example, based on the title, students wondered whether Arthur would be competing with others to read as many books as he could as fast as he could. Then students read the first few sections of text as I monitored and provided help when requested. We stopped after each section to discuss the students' wonderings and reasoning.

PRACTICE: Students continued to read the rest of the story, stopping at designated points to create "I Wonder" Statements and explain their reasoning. (I had placed stop-sign stickers in the texts.) After a brief discussion of their ideas, they continued reading, wondering, and discussing until they finished reading the story.

REREAD, RETELL, AND REFLECT: The students reread the story in partners and engaged in written retellings. I used that time as an opportunity to do a running record with one of the students. Next, we discussed the story and reflected on how creating "I Wonder" Statements helped guide our reading by keeping us engaged with the text. Michael said that he liked "I Wonder" Statements because they helped him say what he was thinking while he was reading.

Student-Facilitated Centers

ART CENTER: The students sketched and labeled wonders from the Arthur stories of their choice. They chose from a variety of mediums to create their illustrations.

LISTENING CENTER: The students selected a partner and listened to various Arthur books on tape. While listening to and reading along with the story, the partners stopped at designated points to discuss the "I Wonder" Statements that they had recorded on their "I Wonder" Bookmarks (see Appendix F, p. 204).

MAKING AND WRITING WORDS: Students engaged in Making and Writing Words by manipulating letters to create words of increasing length and writing them in their Guided Comprehension Journals. Some students also engaged in Making and Writing Words Using Letter Patterns. The first activity concluded with students guessing mystery words taken from Arthur books; the second concluded with students sorting their word cards by word family, number of syllables, or part of speech.

THEME CENTER: Students partner-read Arthur books of their choice, stopping at designated points to record their wonderings and reasonings on their "I Wonder" Bookmarks.

WRITING CENTER: Students worked either with a partner or individually to write and illustrate "I Wonder" stories as sequels to Arthur books they had read. First, the students revisited the Arthur book of their choice. Then they began writing their sequels, using the line "I wonder what will happen next..." Figure 6-1 features Jerry and Sam's story.

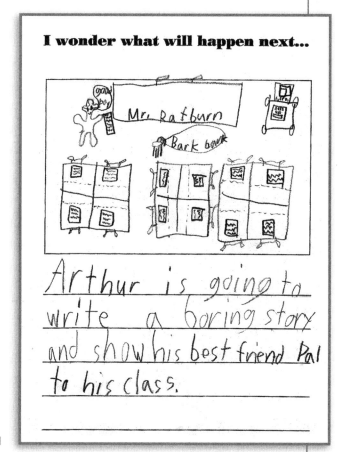

FIGURE 6-1

Student-Facilitated Routines

LITERATURE CIRCLES: The students used their wonderings and reasoning during literature circle as they read a group-selected Arthur text. They used "I Wonder" Statements as a way of questioning what would happen in the story.

CROSS-AGE READING EXPERIENCES: Pairs of students practiced using "I Wonder" Statements with their cross-age partners as they read theme-related texts. Some used "I Wonder" Bookmarks (see Appendix F, p. 204); others did oral wonders.

(STAGE 3) Teacher-Facilitated Whole-Group Reflection

SHARE: We shared applications of "I Wonder" Statements from Stage 2 in small groups. Then we shared selected examples with the whole class.

REFLECT: We reflected on how Self-Questioning and "I Wonder" Statements promoted our engagement with the text and guided our reading.

SET NEW GOALS: The students felt confident of their ability to use "I Wonder" Statements to engage in Self-Questioning when reading stories, so we decided to extend our understanding of "I Wonder" Statements by using them with informational text.

Assessment Options

I observed students in all stages of Guided Comprehension, listening carefully to their wonderings and reasoning. I read and provided feedback on the students' "I Wonder" Bookmarks. I also used their self-assessments, which were very helpful in assessing their ability to self-question. Finally, I completed running records with selected students during our guided small groups.

LESSON 3 Drawing Connections
Strategy: Making Connections

GUIDED COMPREHENSION THEME: Transformational Fairy Tales

STAGE 1 Teacher-Directed Whole-Group Instruction

TEXT: *Cinder Edna* (Jackson, 1994)

EXPLAIN: I explained to the students that good readers make connections to the text before reading, during reading, and after reading, and that we can make text-to-self, text-to-text, and text-to-world connections. I explained that we can express our connections by talking about them, writing about them, or drawing them and that our focus today would be Drawing Connections.

DEMONSTRATE: I introduced the book by retelling the original story of Cinderella with the students' help. Many of the students knew the story very well and freely contributed ideas. Next, I demonstrated Drawing Connections by using a read-aloud, a think-aloud, and an overhead projector. I began by sharing the cover of the book *Cinder Edna*, and I read aloud the first few pages of the story. Then I stopped and used the Drawing Connections blackline (see Appendix F, p. 205) on the overhead to record a

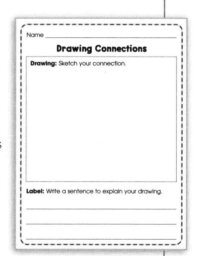

text-to-self connection. I sketched myself cleaning my house, and then I wrote, "Cinderella cleaning her stepmother's house reminds me of how I don't enjoy cleaning my house." I said, "This is a text-to-self connection because it reminds me of something in my life." I read a few more pages and stopped to make a text-to-text connection. I sketched a book cover and wrote, "The Cinderella in this book reminds me of Cinder Elly, a character in another fairy tale I've read. This is a text-to-text connection because I made a connection from one book or text to another book."

GUIDE: I continued reading aloud and stopped at two points during the story to prompt students to make connections. The students worked in partners to draw their connections. We shared and discussed their sketches and sentences, noting what kind of connections they had made. Kendra made a text-to-self connection that said, "Cinderella in her ball gown reminds me of my Halloween costume. I was a princess this year." Mary made a text-to-text connection that said, "Cinder Edna gets married just like Cinderella Penguin did in the book about her."

PRACTICE: I finished reading the story, stopping at two points to have students draw their connections. Students created their own connections and shared them with partners. I circulated around the room to observe students and engage them in conversations about their choices. Then they shared their connections with the class and we discussed the story. Bryan liked that Cinder Edna lived happily ever after because she always found the good in life. He also noticed that Cinderella wasn't very happy because she was always thinking about her troubles. This led to a good discussion about positive thinking and looking for the good in our lives. Brooke noted that she liked making connections because she could talk about the story and about what she knew before she read the story. Roberto said that he liked Drawing Connections because he liked thinking about what the story reminded him of and drawing his ideas.

REFLECT: We reflected on the importance of making connections to the text while we are reading and how it helped us to understand what we read. Then we discussed how we could use Drawing Connections in Stage 2.

STAGE 2   Teacher-Guided Small-Group Instruction

TEXT: *The Three Little Dinosaurs* (Harris, 1999)
(Texts varied according to students' abilities.)

REVIEW: I reviewed the comprehension strategies good readers use and focused on making connections using Drawing Connections.

GUIDE: I introduced the new book that we were going to read, *The Three Little Dinosaurs,* and guided students to draw a connection by using the prompt "This reminds me of..." The students read the first two pages of the text, which tell about the dinosaurs going out to build homes of their own. The first dinosaur pushes dried grass into the shape of a house. Then he sits down to snack and play video games. The other brothers go off on their own to build more stable houses. When the students finished reading that section, they shared the connections that they made. Mark sketched a picture of himself sitting in a chair playing video games. His label read, "This reminds me of when I stay up late playing video games in my chair." Evi sketched a park in which children were playing and she wrote, "The dinosaurs going out on their own reminds me of when my mom lets my friends and me go to the park across the street on our own."

PRACTICE: Students continued to read silently and draw and share connections at designated points. When they had finished reading the story, they shared their final connections, explained which type of connection each was, and discussed the story. Figure 6-2 features Joseph's final connection to *The Three Little Dinosaurs*.

REREAD, RETELL, AND REFLECT: Students reread the story silently and engaged in partner retelling. I used that time to complete a running record with a student I thought might be ready to move to the next level of text. Next, we reflected on the importance of making connections and on how Drawing Connections helped us to better understand the text. Tommy observed that making connections was like "making what I'm reading a part of my life."

FIGURE 6-2

Student-Facilitated Centers and Routines

ART CENTER: A variety of transformational fairy tales were available at this center. Students chose a book to read and used a blackline and various art supplies to engage in Drawing Connections.

LISTENING CENTER: Students listened to the story *Jack and the Meanstalk*, by Brian and Rebecca Wildsmith. They then did Drawing Connections demonstrating text-to-self, text-to-text, or text-to-world connections.

TEACHING CENTER: Students worked with partners to find and circle words containing patterns they knew in a variety of fairy tales that I had left at the center. Each took a turn being the teacher. Then the partners completed Drawing Connections on a transparency.

LITERATURE CIRCLES: The students read fairy tales and used Drawing Connections as the basis for discussing the story.

CROSS-AGE READING EXPERIENCES: Students worked with a cross-age partner and either listened to books on tape or partner-read a transformational fairy tale. Then they drew and labeled their connections.

(STAGE 3) Teacher-Facilitated Whole-Group Reflection

SHARE: Students shared and discussed in small groups their applications of Drawing Connections. Then they shared selected applications with the whole class.

REFLECT: We reflected on how Drawing Connections helped us to make connections with the text, and the students assessed their ability to use this technique. Students also shared their thoughts about how making connections helped us to understand what we read.

SET NEW GOALS: The students decided to extend their goal of making connections to informational texts. They also set a goal to use Drawing Connections in future reading experiences.

Assessment Options

I observed the students in whole-group and small-group instruction. I reviewed students' completed connections to assess their ability to make connections and note the depth of thought evident in the connections. I also read and commented on students' self-assessments.

LESSON 4   Draw and Label Visualizations
Strategy: Visualizing

GUIDED COMPREHENSION THEME: The Rain Forest

(STAGE 1)   Teacher-Directed Whole-Group Instruction

TEXT: *Welcome to the Green House* (Yolen, 1993)

EXPLAIN: I explained that visualizing, one of the comprehension strategies good readers use, involves creating mental pictures based on verbal or written cues. Next, I introduced and explained Draw and Label Visualizations. I explained to the students that we would be using simple sketching to draw the images that we would create in our minds as I read aloud. I modeled some simple lines and shapes and reminded the students that it was important to sketch the images and that we did not need to be great artists to do that.

DEMONSTRATE: I demonstrated Draw and Label Visualizations using a read-aloud of *Welcome to the Green House*, a think-aloud, and a large sheet of chart paper. (See Appendix F, p. 206.) I introduced the book by sharing the title and reading the first page aloud. (I didn't share the cover because I didn't want that picture to influence the images students would be creating.) I thought aloud about the mental images I was creating based on the information I shared. Referring to the title, I said, "I know that a greenhouse is a controlled place for plants to grow. After reading the first page, I know that the story will be discussing what is found in the rain forest. The first page

> Name _____
> **Draw and Label Visualizations**
> **Drawing:** Sketch your visualization.
>
> **Label:** Write a sentence to explain your drawing.

describes vines, trees, and other plants that create the greenhouse. I wonder if the rest of the story will talk about what lives inside this house. After reading the title and the first page, the picture I have in my mind is of many green trees, plants, and vines intertwining with each other." Next, I started sketching on the first of several large pieces of chart paper I had adhered to the chalkboard. I was careful to remind the students that when we draw visualizations, our focus should be on conveying the pictures we have created inside our minds, not worrying about how well we can draw. When I finished sketching, I wrote this sentence as the label: "Many green trees, plants, and vines come together in the rain forest to create a greenhouse." Figure 6-3 features my first Draw and Label Visualization. We briefly discussed my drawing and label. I noted I wrote my label in a complete sentence and reminded the students to do the same. Then I read the next three pages and engaged in Draw and Label Visualizations. I said, "As I read this segment of the text, this is the picture that I created in my mind." I sketched the canopy of many different shades of

FIGURE 6-3

green leaves with a sloth and a monkey in the background. I labeled it: "The sloth and the monkey make their way through the lush green leaves." After that, we briefly discussed my sketch. One student said that after listening to those pages he also visualized different shades of green leaves everywhere with the monkeys and a sloth climbing in it. We discussed how when we visualize, we see images as well as different colors.

GUIDE: I read aloud the next three pages and guided pairs of students to create pictures in their minds and sketch what they were thinking about the story as they were listening to the read-aloud. I monitored this activity, prompting as necessary. The students used paper and colored pencils I had provided. They used think-alouds to share their reasoning with their partners as they individually sketched the images they pictured in their minds and wrote their labels. When they finished, I thought aloud and sketched the mental image I had created as I was reading. I waited to do my sketch because I wanted the students to focus on their visualizations, not copy mine. Then the students and I shared our sketches and our thinking with a partner. Although each sketch was unique, most of us had visualized an array of colorful animals in the rain forest. One of the students drew a visualization that featured some of the animals but mainly focused on lizards crawling everywhere. He said that he could picture the lizards in his mind the best because he has two lizards as pets. This led to a discussion of what influences the mental images we create when reading. I drew attention to the individual nature of visualizations and reinforced the roles that text and prior knowledge play in the personal construction of meaning.

PRACTICE: The students practiced by continuing to create Draw and Label Visualizations and share with their partners, as I continued to read aloud the remaining sections of the book. When I finished reading the book, the students shared their final application of Draw and Label Visualizations with the class. I finished my Draw and Label Visualizations, and then we discussed the story. We talked about the animal and plant life found in the rain forest. We also continued our discussion, based on other lessons in the unit, about why it is important to save the rain forests. We mentioned all of the plant and animal life from the story that would disappear if deforestation continues. Amelia noticed that the story included many descriptive words, and this prompted a great discussion. We talked about how using descriptive words in writing enables the reader to create more vivid and detailed visualizations.

REFLECT: We discussed how Draw and Label Visualizations helped us to think about the story and understand what we were reading. Then we talked about how we could use visualizing when reading different types of text.

(STAGE 2) Teacher-Guided Small-Group Instruction

TEXT: *The Great Kapok Tree* (Cherry, 1990)
(Texts varied according to students' abilities.)

REVIEW: I briefly reviewed the reading comprehension strategies good readers use and focused on visualizing and Draw and Label Visualizations. Next, I introduced the new text and asked the students to sketch and label what they were picturing in their minds as they listened to me share the title and read the first page. I also sketched and labeled my mental image. Then we shared and discussed our Draw and Label Visualizations.

GUIDE: The students partner-read the next section of the book and stopped to draw and label the pictures in their minds. I guided their reading and sketching, prompting as necessary. We followed the same procedure with the next section of the text.

PRACTICE: The students practiced by partner-reading the remaining sections of the book. They stopped twice at designated points to independently draw and label their visualizations. Then the students discussed their Draw and Label Visualizations with their partners. I monitored their discussion, prompting when necessary. Figure 6-4 features Taylor's Draw and Label Visualization for *The Great Kapok Tree*.

REREAD, RETELL, REFLECT: The students engaged in a second reading of the text by whisper-reading. I used this as an opportunity to listen to the students read independently, and I completed a running record with one of the students. Then we engaged in an oral retelling of the story. Finally, we discussed how the visualized images belonged to each reader, and how they were sometimes similar and sometimes very different from the images of others. We also talked about how drawing and labeling our visualizations helped us comprehend the content of the story. One student said, "Making pictures in my head as I read the story helped me to remember what happened in the story." Another student said, "It made the story more interesting when I was creating pictures inside of my head and helped me to make connections. When I was picturing the monkeys in my head, it made me think of when I saw monkeys at the zoo." These reflections prompted other students to reflect and make connections. We shared and discussed the students' completed Draw and Label Visualizations.

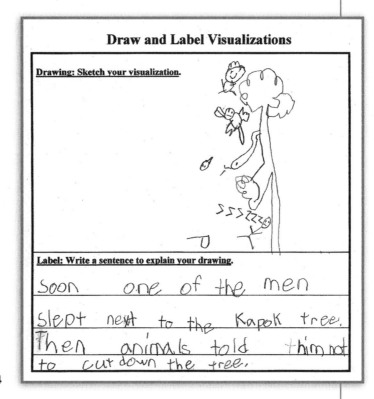

Draw and Label Visualizations

Drawing: Sketch your visualization.

Label: Write a sentence to explain your drawing.

Soon one of the men
slept next to the Kapok tree.
Then animals told him not
to cut down the tree.

FIGURE 6-4

Student-Facilitated Centers and Routines

LISTENING CENTER: Students worked in pairs to listen to rain forest books various parent volunteers had put on tape for us. The tapes stopped at two points, so the students could engage in Draw and Label Visualizations and share with their partner.

THEME CENTER: A variety of theme-based books were available at this center. Students chose a book to read and used a blackline (see Appendix F, p. 206) to complete and share at least two Draw and Label Visualizations based on their reading.

LITERATURE CIRCLES: The students read books about rain forests and created Draw and Label Visualizations as they read. These were shared in the discussion circle that followed.

CROSS-AGE READING EXPERIENCES: Students worked with cross-age partners to read and create Draw and Label Visualizations. They stopped at various points during the reading to sketch and label their visualizations and to share and discuss them.

STAGE 3 — Teacher-Facilitated Whole-Group Reflection

SHARE: Students shared with partners the Draw and Label Visualizations they had completed in Stage 2. Then they shared selected applications with the whole group.

REFLECT: We reflected on how using Draw and Label Visualizations helped us to share our mental images and reflect on what we saw in our minds as we were reading. The students felt they could successfully use this visualizing technique, and a variety of assessments supported their thinking.

SET NEW GOALS: The students decided to extend their goal of integrating visualizing into their repertoire of strategies by learning how to use Draw and Label Visualizations in science and social studies.

Assessment Options

I observed the students in whole group and during our guided small group. I commented on students' Draw and Label Visualizations and the self-assessments they completed in the centers and routines. I also completed several running records in the guided small-group setting.

LESSON 5 Bookmark Technique
Strategy: Monitoring

GUIDED COMPREHENSION THEME: Great Inventors: The Wright Brothers

STAGE 1 Teacher-Directed Whole-Group Instruction

TEXT: *First to Fly* (Busby, 2002)

EXPLAIN: I began by explaining what monitoring is and how we need to constantly ask ourselves "Does this make sense?" as we read. Then I explained one way to do this is by using Bookmark Technique. I explained that we could bookmark our ideas while we read and after we read. I explained that we would be using four bookmarks, as I held up the Bookmark Technique blacklines we would be using (see Appendix F, pp. 212-213). The first would ask what we thought was the most interesting part of the text. The second bookmark would ask which part of the text was confusing when we read it. The third bookmark would ask what word we thought the whole class should discuss, and the fourth bookmark would ask what illustration, chart, map, or graph helped us to understand what we read.

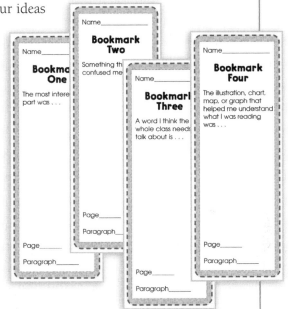

DEMONSTRATE: To demonstrate, I used the book *First to Fly*, by Peter Busby. I showed on the overhead projector the bookmarks we would be using and explained that we would be using Bookmark Technique to help us make sense of what we read. Using a read-aloud and a think-aloud, I read the prologue from the book *First to Fly* and said to the students, "I think the most interesting part of the prologue is that they became interested in flight with a toy they called 'bat.'" I explained to the students that I would draw a sketch of the "bat" and write a sentence about it on the bookmark. I was careful to demonstrate that every time we complete a bookmark, we write in the space provided on the bookmark the number of the page on which we found the information.

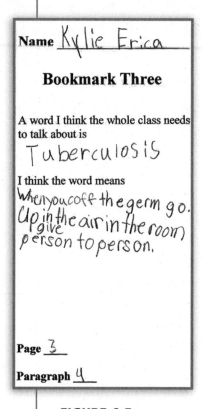

FIGURE 6-5

GUIDE: Students worked with partners as I read the next few pages. When I stopped reading, I guided the pairs as they decided what word they thought the whole group needed to discuss. Then they wrote and/or sketched on their bookmarks the words and what they thought they meant. We discussed the students' bookmarks and added their words to our word wall. Figure 6-5 shows Kylie and Erica's bookmarks.

PRACTICE: I finished reading the text and stopped to provide time for the students to sketch and write on their bookmarks. This time, they were working on two bookmarks: One focused on an illustration that helped them with their reading, the other on something they found confusing. I walked around the room to observe and listen as the students completed their work. Then we discussed the bookmarks.

REFLECT: We talked about why it is important to ask ourselves "Does this make sense?" as we read and how using Bookmark Technique helps us to do that. Eddie said, "I like doing the bookmarks because it helps me to remember what I read and I like that we can write or sketch on the bookmarks."

(STAGE 2) Teacher-Guided Small-Group Instruction

TEXT: *My Brothers' Flying Machine* (Yolen, 2003)
(Texts varied according to students' abilities.)

REVIEW: First I reviewed the comprehension strategies good readers use to make sense of text and then I focused students on monitoring by using Bookmark Technique.

GUIDE: In our group we talked about what we knew about flight in general. Then I introduced the text by sharing the title and engaging the students in a picture walk. Next, I guided the students to whisper-read the first four pages of the text, listening to them as they read to check for fluency. As they read, I encouraged them to complete a bookmark. (The students didn't include paragraph numbers because the book was written in verse.)

PRACTICE: Students continued to whisper-read the text and sketch or write on their bookmarks. I continued to monitor through this process.

REREAD, RETELL, AND REFLECT: We discussed the students' completed bookmarks (Tiana's bookmarks are featured in Figure 6-6) and the students reread the sections of the text that related to their bookmarks. Then we did an oral retelling of the story. Finally, we reflected on how bookmarks help us understand and make sense of what we read. We also talked about how we could use Bookmark Technique when reading other texts.

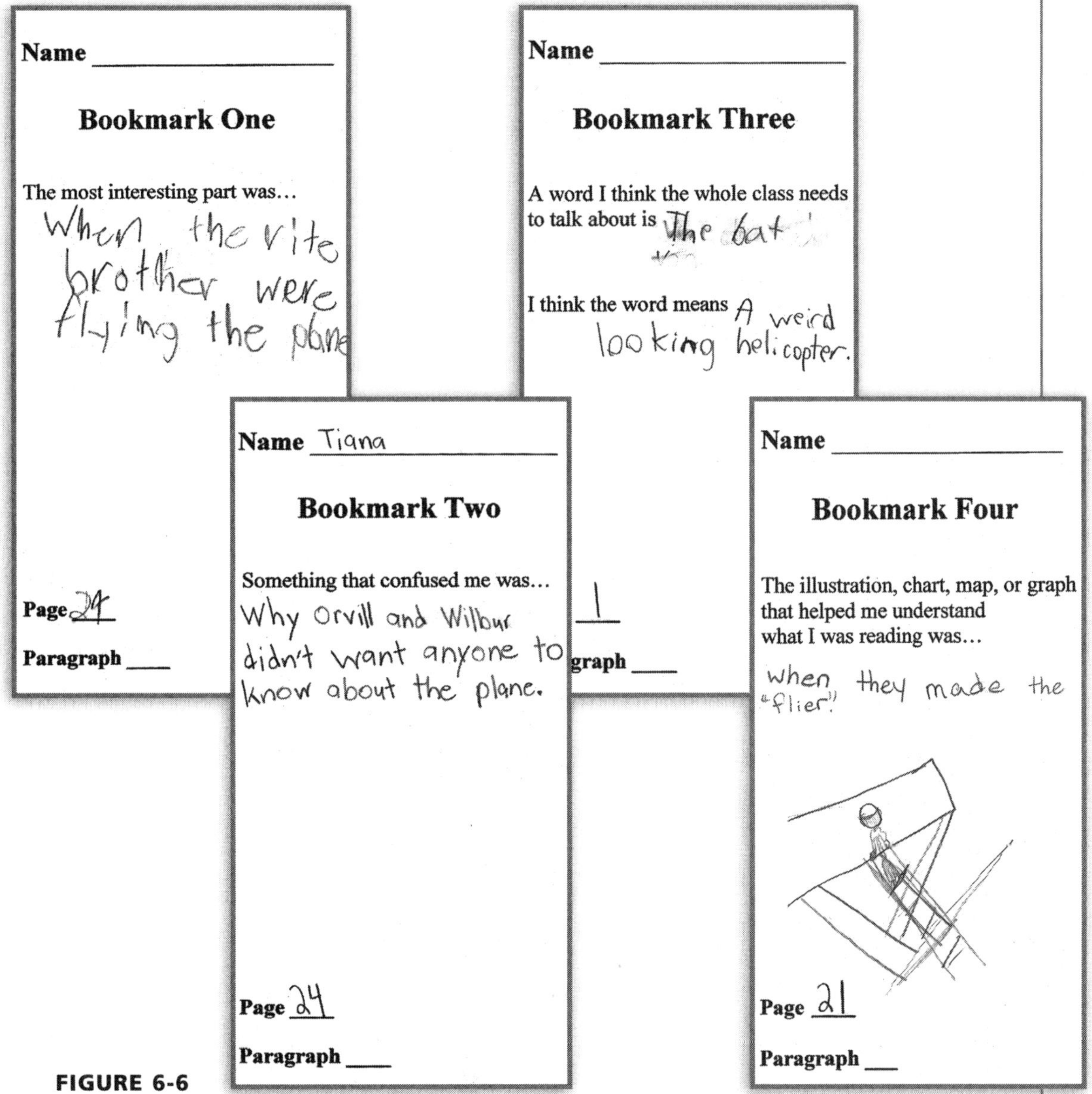

Name _____

Bookmark One

The most interesting part was…
When the rite brother were flying the plane

Page 24

Paragraph ____

Name _____

Bookmark Three

A word I think the whole class needs to talk about is The bat

I think the word means A weird looking helicopter.

Name Tiana _____

Bookmark Two

Something that confused me was…
Why Orvill and Wilbur didn't want anyone to know about the plane.

Page 24

Paragraph ____

Name _____

Bookmark Four

The illustration, chart, map, or graph that helped me understand what I was reading was…
when they made the "flier".

Page 21

Paragraph ____

FIGURE 6-6

Student-Facilitated Centers and Routine

ART CENTER: Students read various books and articles about flight and completed their bookmarks by sketching.

THEME CENTER: I placed numerous books and articles about flight at this center. Pairs of students worked together and read the text using partner reading patterns. As they read, the students completed Bookmark Technique.

LITERATURE CIRCLES: The students used Bookmark Technique as they read their selected text. The discussion director used the completed bookmarks to spark discussion.

(STAGE 3) Teacher-Facilitated Whole-Group Reflection

SHARE: The students shared their bookmarks from Stage 2 in small groups and then we discussed their work in whole group.

REFLECT: We reflected on how Bookmark Technique helped us make sense of what we read. Gracie said she liked using Bookmark Technique because "when I was reading I was thinking about what I would write on my bookmarks and when I was done reading, the bookmarks helped me to remember important ideas to share when we talk about the book." The other students agreed. Kevin said, "That's what bookmarks do. They help us to remember what we think about the story."

SET NEW GOALS: Finally, we set goals based on how well we could use Bookmark Technique and decided that we would expand our understanding of monitoring by using Bookmark Technique with other genres.

Assessment Options

I observed students during all three stages of the Guided Comprehension lesson. I also assessed the students' completed bookmarks and made note of the students' contributions to discussion.

LESSON 6 Draw and Label Retelling
Strategy: Summarizing

GUIDED COMPREHENSION THEME: Ducks, Ducks, and More Ducks!

STAGE 1 Teacher-Directed Whole-Group Instruction

TEXT: *Duck for President* (Cronin, 2004)

EXPLAIN: I explained that when we summarize we include only the important information from what we have been reading. I explained that what is important information in a story is different from the information that is important in biographies or other types of informational texts.

I explained that the purpose of retelling a story is to recount what happened in the story in order, including the characters, where the story took place, what happened in the story, and how the story ended. I reminded the students that much like many of the ideas we had learned, retellings could be oral, written, drawn, dramatized, or sung. Then I explained that our focus today would be the Draw and Label Retelling.

DEMONSTRATE: To start the demonstration, I divided a large piece of butcher paper into four parts. I labeled each section so that it looked like a very large version of the Draw and Label Retelling blackline (see Appendix F, p. 214). I explained that we would be using *Duck for President*, which I had read to the students earlier in the day, as the focus of our retelling. I used a think-aloud as I recalled and drew the elements of the story. I began by thinking aloud about who was in the story. I used the title and cover as prompts and said, "I remember that Farmer Brown, Duck, and all of the other farm animals were in the story." Then I drew a picture of the characters in the appropriate section of the organizer and wrote a sentence to label my drawing. I wrote, "Farmer Brown, Duck, and other farm animals were in the story." I continued to model by thinking aloud as I looked back through the book to find out about the setting. When I found the necessary information, I drew a picture of the setting in the designated box. Then I wrote this sentence to label my drawing: "The story took place on a farm, in a town, and in Washington, D.C."

Name _____

Draw and Label Retelling

Who? Draw:	Where? Draw:
Label: _____	Label: _____
What happened? Draw:	How did it end? Draw:
Label: _____	Label: _____

GUIDE: I continued to the "What happened?" box and guided the students in completing the box. The students worked in small groups and drew what happened in the designated box on forms I had provided for them. Then each group wrote a sentence to label their drawing and shared their responses with the class. One group wrote, "Duck didn't like how the farmer, the governor, or the President did things, so he did their jobs." After discussing their efforts, I quickly sketched what happened on the large graphic and wrote a sentence to label my drawing.

PRACTICE: Students practiced by completing the "How did it end?" box in their small groups. They shared their drawings and sentences with the class and, based on their responses, I completed the Draw and Label Retelling I had posted on the board. (See Figure 6-7 for the completed Draw and Label Retelling for *Duck for President*.) Then we used the information on the organizer to create a whole-class oral retelling of *Duck for President*.

REFLECT: After retelling the story, we talked about how summarizing helps us to remember the important information about what we have read. One of the students observed that drawing what was important made summarizing fun. Another commented that the Draw and Label Retelling blackline (see Appendix F, p. 214) was like a map telling us what to do next. We concluded our discussion by sharing ideas about how we could use the Draw and Label Retelling in Stage 2.

FIGURE 6-7

STAGE 2 — Teacher-Guided Small-Group Instruction

TEXTS: *Oh, Ducky!* (Slonim, 2003)

The Web Files (Palatini, 2001)

(Texts varied according to students' abilities.)

REVIEW: I began by reviewing summarizing, story elements, and strategies good readers use.

GUIDE: I introduced the text and guided the students through the reading of *Oh, Ducky!* I assigned each student in the group a specific story element (characters, setting, what happened, how the story ended) to draw and label as part of our group Draw and Label Retelling. They shared their ideas with a partner and then with the group. I pasted their work onto our group Draw and Label Retelling blackline (see Appendix F, p. 214). Then we retold the story based on the information each group member had provided (see Figure 6-8 for the guided group Draw and Label Retelling).

PRACTICE: Students practiced with a partner by reading *The Web Files* and using the Draw and Label Retelling blackline to record the important elements of the story. Then they used the completed organizer to retell the story orally. I observed the students' progress during this activity.

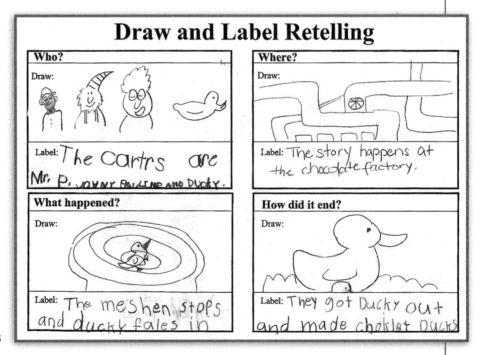

FIGURE 6-8

REREAD, RETELL, AND REFLECT: When students finished rereading the story, we engaged in an oral group retelling. Then we talked about the different duck books we had read, and how the Draw and Label Retelling extended our understanding and enjoyment of these books.

Student-Facilitated Centers and Routine

ART CENTER: Students used vibrant markers and the Draw and Label Retelling organizer to retell *Click, Clack, Moo: Cows That Type,* by Doreen Cronin, and other duck-related books.

WRITING CENTER: Students worked with partners and wrote flip-book stories about *Tuff Fluff: The Case of Duckie's Missing Brain.* Then they completed Draw and Label Retellings of their stories. Matt and Stephanie's flip-book was titled *Tuff Fluff: The Case of Duckie's Missing Beak.* Cody and Beth's flip book was titled *Tuff Fluff Finds a Friend.*

LITERATURE CIRCLES: I adapted the Literature Circle by limiting the roles to literary luminary and discussion director. One group of students read *Giggle, Giggle, Quack,* by Doreen Cronin and used it as the basis of their discussion. Then they created a group Draw and Label Retelling.

STAGE 3   Teacher-Facilitated Whole-Group Reflection

SHARE: Students shared in small groups the retellings they created in Stage 2 of Guided Comprehension. I monitored this and we engaged in a whole-group sharing of the stories they wrote in the Writing Center. Students then displayed their books in our Duck Gallery.

REFLECT: We reflected on how well we could summarize and retell stories using the Draw and Label Retelling and how much we enjoyed drawing and labeling. We also reflected on how summarizing improved our understanding of what we read.

SET NEW GOALS: We decided we were good at using the Draw and Label Retelling and that we would extend our goal of knowing how to summarize by learning how to summarize informational texts.

Assessment Options

I used observation, students' completed retellings, students' stories, and student self-reflections as assessments.

LESSON 7   Discussion Web
Strategy: Evaluating

GUIDED COMPREHENSION THEME: Living in Our World

STAGE 1   Teacher-Directed Whole-Group Instruction

TEXTS: *H is for Home Run* (Herzog, 2004)

Mama Played Baseball (Adler, 2003)

EXPLAIN: I began by asking the students what an opinion was. They responded with ideas such as "It's what someone thinks" and "It is an idea someone has." I explained what evaluating was and how we use it to make decisions about what we are reading. Then I explained that one way to evaluate is to use a Discussion Web, which I displayed on chart paper. I explained that Discussion Webs would help us to evaluate authors' ideas, think about topics from two different perspectives, and reach our own conclusions.

DEMONSTRATE: To demonstrate, I used the books *H is for Home Run* by Brad Herzog and *Mama Played Baseball* by David A. Adler. Prior to reading the books, I thought aloud and questioned, "Who plays baseball?" I thought aloud about several responses including Derek Jeter, Mike Piazza, boys in the class, and girls play softball. Next, I introduced and read aloud the book *H is for Home Run* and directed the students' attention to the enlarged Discussion Web blackline I had placed on the front board (see Appendix F, p. 215). I had chosen to read this book first because it featured mostly boys and men playing baseball. I placed the question "Should only men be allowed to play professional baseball?" in the center box of the Discussion Web blackline. I used a think-aloud to begin adding

information to the Discussion Web. I said, "I noticed the book said that the best player was a man: Babe Ruth, so I will add that information to the Yes column." Then I said, "Basically, all of the illustrations feature men or boys. I will note that in the Yes column." I continued to think aloud and add information to our Discussion Web.

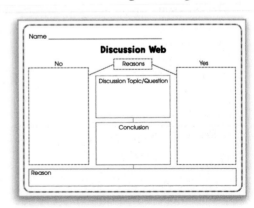

GUIDE: Next, I introduced and read aloud the book *Mama Played Baseball*, which supported the opposite point of view. I guided the students to suggest information that we should include on our Discussion Web. Much of this information was placed in the No column. Ideas they added included *the woman in the book was on a team*; *there was a women's league during WWII*; *women played in stadiums and wore uniforms*; and *women were paid to play*.

PRACTICE: To practice evaluating and completing a Discussion Web, I had the students work in pairs to find more examples to support the Yes and No columns on the Discussion Web. Next, the pairs of students discussed whether only men should play professional baseball. They worked together to develop their responses to the question "Should only men be allowed to play professional baseball?" The overwhelming majority of the pairs concluded that both men and women should play professional baseball. Students cited the history of the women's league and other sports, such as basketball, in which both women and men play on professional teams. Rich and Beth said, "Anyone who works hard, practices, and becomes a great player should be able to play on a professional team." Judy and Miguel said, "It shouldn't just be men. There are lots of things in *Mama Played Baseball* that show that women can be good players too." Our completed Discussion Web is featured in Figure 6-9.

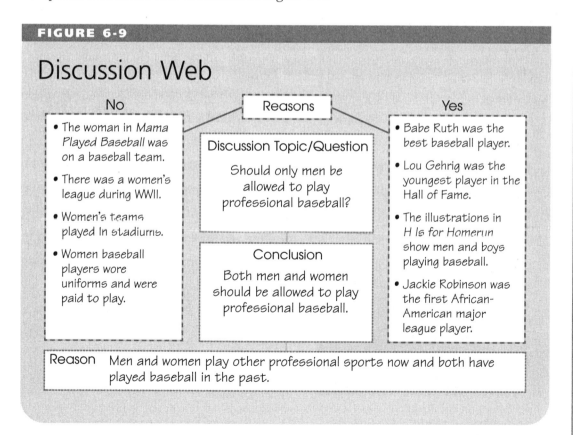

FIGURE 6-9

Discussion Web

No — **Reasons** — **Yes**

No
- The woman in *Mama Played Baseball* was on a baseball team.
- There was a women's league during WWII.
- Women's teams played in stadiums.
- Women baseball players wore uniforms and were paid to play.

Discussion Topic/Question
Should only men be allowed to play professional baseball?

Conclusion
Both men and women should be allowed to play professional baseball.

Yes
- Babe Ruth was the best baseball player.
- Lou Gehrig was the youngest player in the Hall of Fame.
- The illustrations in *H Is for Homerun* show men and boys playing baseball.
- Jackie Robinson was the first African-American major league player.

Reason   Men and women play other professional sports now and both have played baseball in the past.

REFLECT: We reflected on how using a Discussion Web helped us to look at both sides of an issue and form an opinion. Then we talked about how it is important to look at the facts on both sides of an issue before we make decisions and how important it is to continually evaluate what the author is trying to tell us. It was also wonderful to see how quickly the students took ownership of the vocabulary used in this discussion about baseball. Of course, our school is near Yankee Stadium, and the students are great fans!

(STAGE 2) Teacher-Guided Small-Group Instruction

TEXT: *Martin's Big Words* (Rappaport, 2001)
(Texts varied according to students' abilities.)

REVIEW: I reviewed the comprehension strategies that good readers use and focused on evaluating using Discussion Webs. I reminded the students that by evaluating a text, we can make informed decisions about a topic. Next, I reviewed with them the Discussion Web and how it is used to make decisions and form opinions.

GUIDE: I introduced and guided the students' reading of *Martin's Big Words*. I monitored as they read. After they finished reading the selection, I guided them to begin completing the Discussion Web based on the question "Did Dr. Martin Luther King, Jr., help solve problems in our country?"

PRACTICE: To practice, I had students find additional information to support each side of the issue. Then the students worked in pairs to develop their conclusions. Later the entire group discussed the question, came to a conclusion, and offered reasons to support our thinking. Our completed Discussion Web appears in Figure 6-10.

REFLECT: We reflected on how using a Discussion Web helped us to evaluate the text, look at an issue from both sides, and make an informed decision.

FIGURE 6-10

Discussion Web

Reasons

Problems

- White Only signs in the South meant only white people could drink from water fountains or eat in restaurants.

- Black people had to sit in the back of the bus.

- Rosa Parks was arrested for not giving up her seat on the bus.

- Black people were put in jail, beaten, and killed.

Discussion Topic/Question

Did Dr. Martin Luther King, Jr., help solve problems in our country?

Conclusion

Dr. King did help to solve problems in our country.

What Dr. King Did

- Dr. King said that all people can be great.

- Black people did not ride busses until they could sit anywhere on the busses.

- Dr. King led peaceful protest marches.

- Dr. King said he had a dream about people living together.

- Dr. King won the Nobel Peace Prize.

Reason Dr. King had a dream and helped to make our country a better place to live by giving speeches, marching with the people, and believing that we could all live together.

Student-Facilitated Centers

ART CENTER: Students used a variety of mediums to create posters representing their positions on topics we had already addressed through Discussion Webs. They hung their work in our Art Gallery.

THEME CENTER: I placed several theme-related informational articles and Discussion Web graphic organizers at this center. I grouped the articles and blacklines together and provided a question to get the students started. Then students worked in pairs to read the articles and complete the related Discussion Webs.

WRITING CENTER: Students worked with partners to write and illustrate persuasive paragraphs about which side they would support in debatable circumstances. Referencing books I had recently read to the students, I provided several possible prompts, ranging from who was at fault—the pigs or the wolf in *The True Story of the 3 Little Pigs!* (Scieszka, 1996)—to whether it was fair for coal mines to employ young children, as reported in *Growing Up in Coal Country* (Bartoletti, 1996).

Student-Facilitated Routines

CROSS-AGE READING EXPERIENCES: Students read with cross-age partners, discussed what they had read, and completed Discussion Webs.

LITERATURE CIRCLES: We adapted the Literature Circles, and instead of all the students reading the same book, the students read informational articles from a variety of sources. As they read, they added information to their Discussion Web. Then they used the Discussion Web format to discuss the issue.

(STAGE 3) Teacher-Facilitated Whole-Group Reflection

SHARE: Students shared the Discussion Webs they completed during Stage 2 of Guided Comprehension. Next, students shared in small group the persuasive paragraphs they had written. Finally, we took a walk through the class gallery to review the students' posters.

REFLECT: We reflected on how well we could evaluate ideas using the Discussion Web and how important it was always to have reasons for our thinking.

SET NEW GOALS: We decided to continue learning about evaluating by learning how to use Discussion Webs with current events.

Assessment Options

I used observation, the Discussion Webs students completed, and student self-reflections as assessments. I also assessed a few students by doing running records during the guided reading groups.

Final Thoughts on This Chapter

The lessons in this chapter integrated research findings and current beliefs about best practice in teaching reading comprehension strategies. The research-based Guided Comprehension Model for the Primary Grades provided a format that integrated direct and guided instruction and independent practice. Narrative and informational texts at a variety of levels and a variety of modes of reader response were also used. Reflection and informal assessments permeated the lessons. The lessons were designed to facilitate students' learning the strategies, so they can build a repertoire of strategies and regulate their use.

It's important to note that although the lessons featured in this chapter were taught at particular grade levels, they can be adapted to accommodate other levels and needs. For example, first-grade teachers taught Lessons 1 and 2, second-grade teachers taught Lessons 3, 4, and 6, and third-grade teachers taught Lessons 5 and 7. But if students at other levels had not mastered particular reading comprehension strategies, the lessons could be
adapted to teach them. Students develop at their own rates, and their needs for different skills and strategies vary. Ideas to adapt the lessons to accommodate English Language Learners, struggling readers, and special needs students include changing the level of the texts, adding more modeling and demonstration, providing more examples or focusing on fewer examples, providing time for more guided instruction or independent practice, and changing the level of word choice or questioning. Most of the lessons address skills and strategies that develop over time and continue to need reinforcement.

In the next section, we conclude our work by reflecting on teaching reading in current times.

What can we read to learn more about teaching comprehension?

Farstrup, A., & Samuels, J. (Eds.) (2002). *What research has to say about reading instruction.* Newark, DE: International Reading Association.

Kamil, M. L., Mosenthal, P. B., Pearson, P. D., & Barr, R. (Eds.) (2000). *Handbook of reading research* (Vol. 3). Mahwah, NJ: Erlbaum.

McLaughlin, M. (2003). *Guided comprehension in the primary grades.* Newark, DE: International Reading Association.

Continuing the Journey

As reading professionals, we know that teaching is a lifelong learning experience and we fully embrace it. We constantly question what we know and how we can use it to benefit our students. We are always looking for new ways to motivate them, and we are constantly searching for up-to-the-minute information that will help them to learn to the best of their abilities. Teaching phonemic awareness, phonics, fluency, vocabulary, and comprehension will help us do that.

As we have noted at various points throughout this book, none of these "critical elements of literacy" are new to us. What is new is the current emphasis on teaching them, and from our perspective that is a good thing. As reading teachers, we have all known the joy of hearing a child read for the first time. We have heard students' fluency develop because they were nurtured by models of fluent reading. We understand that vocabulary is an essential component of comprehension and we know that the latest research tells us that primary-grade students are very capable of learning comprehension strategies.

We are living in an age of possibility. We know that teaching the critical elements of reading will help our students. The challenges that remain are time for and access to meaningful professional development, funding for classroom support (reading specialists, literacy coaches, aides), funding for innovative materials and the space in which to use them, and limiting the assessments we give to meaningful measures that will provide information about our students and inform our teaching.

And yes, as we try to keep pace with these challenges, we may occasionally need to be reminded that we, as teachers, are the single most important influence on our students' learning (International Reading Association, 2000; National Commission on Teaching and America's Future, 1997; Ruddell, 2004). We think that information cannot be emphasized enough.

In our introduction, we thanked you for joining us in our quest to help our students reach their greatest potential. We thank you now for continuing to honor that commitment.

Appendix A

Books that Promote Phonemic Awareness, Phonics, and Fluency

Adams, P. (1990). *This is the house that Jack built*. New York: Child's Play.

Andreae, G. (2003). *K is for kissing a cool kangaroo*. New York: Orchard Books.

Ashman, L. (2002). *Can you make a piggy giggle?* New York: Dutton.

Axtell, D. (1999). *We're going on a lion hunt*. New York: Henry Holt.

Bennett, J. (1987). *Noisy poems*. Hong Kong: Oxford University Press.

Brown, M. W. (1993). *Four fur feet*. New York: Doubleday.

Bruss, D. (2001). *Book! Book! Book!* New York: Arthur A. Levine.

Bynum, J. (1999). *Altoona Baboona*. New York: Harcourt.

Calmenson, S. (1998). *The teeny tiny teacher*. New York: Scholastic.

Carle, E. (2002). *Does a kangaroo have a mother, too?* New York: HarperCollins.

Carle, E. (2002). *"Slowly, slowly, slowly," said the sloth*. New York: Penguin Putnam.

Catalanotto, P. (2002). *Matthew A.B.C.* New York: Simon & Schuster.

Christelow, E. (1989). *Five little monkeys jumping on the bed*. New York: Clarion Books.

Christelow, E. (1991). *Five little monkeys sitting in a tree*. New York: Trumpet.

Colandro, L. (2002). *There was an old lady who swallowed a bat!* New York: Scholastic.

Cowley, J. (2003). *Mrs. Wishy-Washy's farm*. New York: Philomel Books.

deRegniers, B., Moore, E., White, M., & Carr, J. (1988). *Sing a song of popcorn*. New York: Scholastic.

Deming, A. G. (1994). *Who is tapping at my window?* New York: Penguin.

Edwards, P. (1995). *Four famished foxes and Fosdyke*. New York: Harper Trophy.

Ehlert, L. (1989). *Eating the alphabet: Fruits and vegetables from A to Z*. San Diego, CA: Harcourt Brace Jovanovich.

Fajerman, D. (2002). *How to speak moo!* Hauppauge, NY: Barron's Educational Series.

Freedman, C. (2001). *Where's your smile, crocodile?* Atlanta, GA: Peachtree.

Fuge, C. (2002). *I know a rhino*. New York: Sterling.

Gordon, J. (1991). *Six sleepy sheep*. New York: Puffin.

Jackson, A. (1997). *I know an old lady who swallowed a pie*. New York: Penguin Group.

Kuskin, K. (1990). *Roar and more*. New York: Harper Trophy.

Lewison, W. (1992). *Buzz said the bee*. New York: Scholastic.

Low, A. (2004). *Aunt Lucy went to buy a hat*. New York: HarperCollins.

Martin, B. (1967). *Brown bear, brown bear what do you see?* New York: Henry Holt.

Martin, B. (1997). *Polar bear, polar bear, what do you hear?* New York: Henry Holt.

Martin, B. (2003). *Panda bear, panda bear, what do you see?* New York: Henry Holt.

Miranda, A. (1998). *To market, to market.* New York: Scholastic.

Mitton, T. (2001). *Down by the cool of the pool.* New York: Orchard Books.

Numeroff, L. (1999). *Sometimes I wonder if poodles like noodles.* New York: Simon & Schuster.

Obligado, L. (1983). *Faint frogs feeling feverish and other terrifically tantalizing tongue twisters.* New York: Viking.

Ochs, C. P. (1991). *Moose on the loose.* Minneapolis, MN: Carolrhoda Books.

Parry, C. (1991). *Zoomerang-a-boomerang.* New York: Puffin Books.

Patz, N. (1983). *Moses supposes his toeses are roses.* San Diego, CA: Harcourt Brace Jovanovich.

Prelutsky, J. (1986). *Read-aloud rhymes for the very young.* New York: Knopf.

Prelutsky, J. (1989). *Poems of A. Nonny Mouse.* New York: Knopf.

Robetch, L. (2001). *Ook the book.* San Francisco, CA: Chronicle.

Rosen, M. (1997). *We're going on a bear hunt.* New York: Little Simon.

Roth, C. (2002). *The little school bus.* New York: North-South Books.

Sendak, M. (1990). *Alligators all around: An alphabet.* New York: Harper Trophy.

Seuss, Dr. (1965). *Fox in socks.* New York: Random House.

Seuss, Dr. (1974). *There's a wocket in my pocket.* New York: Random House.

Seuss, Dr. (1976). *One fish, two fish, red fish, blue fish.* New York: Random House.

Seuss, Dr. (1996). *Dr. Seuss's ABC.* New York: Random House.

Seuss, Dr. (1996). *Mr. Brown can moo! Can you? Dr. Seuss's book of wonderful noises.* New York: Random House.

Shaw, N. (1986). *Sheep in a jeep.* Boston: Houghton Mifflin.

Shaw, N. (1991). *Sheep in a shop.* Boston: Houghton Mifflin.

Shaw, N. (1995). *Sheep out to eat.* Boston: Houghton Mifflin.

Shaw, N. (1997). *Sheep trick or treat.* Boston: Houghton Mifflin.

Shulman, L. (2002). *Old MacDonald had a woodshop.* New York: G.P. Putnam's Sons.

Slate, J. (1996). *Miss Bindergarten gets ready for kindergarten.* New York: Dutton.

Slate, J. (1996). *Miss Bindergarten celebrates the 100th day.* New York: Puffin.

Slate, J. (1996). *Miss Bindergarten takes a field trip.* New York: Dutton.

Taback, S. (1997). *There was an old lady who swallowed a fly.* New York: Viking.

Weeks, S. (1998). *Mrs. McNosh hangs up her wash.* New York: Harper Trophy.

Wilson, K. (2003). *Bear wants more.* New York: Margaret K. McElderry Books.

Wood, A. (1984). *The napping house.* Orlando, FL: Harcourt.

Yolen, J. (1997). *The three bears rhyme book.* San Diego, CA: Harcourt.

© McLaughlin & Fisher. (2005). *Research-Based Reading Lessons for K–3.* New York: Scholastic.

Appendix B

Ideas for Teaching Phonemic Awareness

There are numerous practical and motivational ways to teach different aspects of phonemic awareness. Frequently hearing, saying, and creating rhymes; manipulating syllables; and singing songs adapted to promote phonemic awareness are among many found to be effective.

What follows is a sampling of teaching ideas. For a more extensive list of ideas for teaching phonemic awareness, see the lessons and resources at the conclusion of Chapter 2. For other fun and engaging literature to use when teaching phonemic awareness, see Appendix A.

Rhymes

Read a variety of rhymes to students and encourage them to say or sing them along with you. *Read-Aloud Rhymes for the Very Young*, compiled by Jack Prelutsky and illustrated by Marc Brown, is one example of a text that provides a wide variety of rhymes to share. Students will also enjoy developing their understanding of rhyme by frequently saying classic nursery rhymes such as "Jack and Jill" and "Humpty Dumpty."

Read to students books with rhyming texts and, after students become familiar with the rhyme scheme, pause and encourage them to predict the next rhyming word. Nancy Shaw's sheep books—*Sheep in a Jeep*, *Sheep in a Shop*, *Sheep Out to Eat*, *Sheep Trick or Treat*— are examples of texts that would work well. See Appendix A for other text suggestions.

Syllable Manipulation

"Clap, Clap, Clap Your Hands" (cues) can be adapted for language manipulation (Yopp, 1992). This version of "Clap, Clap, Clap Your Hands" encourages blending syllables. The first two verses below are part of the original song; the last two verses are an adaptation (Yopp & Yopp, 2000).

> Clap, clap, clap your hands,
> Clap your hands together.
> Clap, clap, clap your hands,
> Clap your hands together.
>
> Snap, snap, snap, your fingers.
> Snap your fingers together.
> Snap, snap, snap your fingers.
> Snap your fingers together.

Say, say, say these parts.

Say these parts together.

Say, say, say these parts,

Say these parts together:

Teacher: moun (pause) tain (children respond: "mountain!").

Teacher: love (pause) ly (children respond: "lovely!")

Teacher: un (pause) der (children respond: "under!")

Teacher: tea (pause) cher (children respond: "teacher!")

Phoneme Manipulation

Singing traditional songs, with lyrics revised to promote phonemic awareness, can promote a variety of aspects of phonemic awareness, including sound isolation, sound addition or deletion, and full segmentation. Yopp (1992) suggests the following:

SOUND ISOLATION ACTIVITY: Children may be given a word and asked to tell what sound occurs at the beginning, middle, or end of the word.

"Old MacDonald Had a Farm"

What's the sound that starts these words:

Turtle, time, and teeth?

/t/ is the sound that starts these words:

Turtle, time, and teeth.

With a /t/, /t/ here, and a /t/, /t/ there,

Here a /t/, there a /t/, everywhere a /t/, /t/.

/t/ is the sound that starts these words:

Turtle, time, and teeth. (Chicken, chin, and cheek)

SOUND ADDITION OR DELETION ACTIVITY: Students may add or substitute sounds in words in familiar songs.

"Row, Row, Row Your Boat"

Row, row, row your boat

Gently down the stream.

Merrily, merrily, merrily, merrily

Life is but a dream.

© McLaughlin & Fisher. (2005). *Research-Based Reading Lessons for K–3*. New York: Scholastic.

(Berrily, berrily, berrily, berrily)

(Derrily, derrily, derrily, derrily)

(Terrily, terrily, terrily, terrily)

(Werrily, werrily, werrily, werrily)

(Zerrily, zerrily, zerrily, zerrily)

Full Segmentation:

"Twinkle, Twinkle, Little Star"

Listen, listen to my word,

Then tell me the sounds you heard: face

/f/ is one sound

/a/ is two,

/s/ is the last sound its true.

Thanks for listening to my words,

And telling me the sounds you heard.

Scavenger Hunt (Letters)

Children work in teams of three. Each team has a bag. The outside of the bag has a letter and a picture of an object that begins with that letter. For instance, one team receives a bag with the letter *M* on it and a picture of a monkey; another team receives a bag with letter *S* on it and a picture of a snake. Children then set off on a scavenger hunt to find objects in the classroom that begin with their target sound. Provide enough time for the children to be successful, then bring them together to share their target sound and the objects they found (Yopp & Yopp, 2000).

Ideas for Teaching Phonics

There are numerous ideas available for teaching phonics. *Words Their Way* (Bear, Invernizzi, Templeton, & Johnston, 2000) and *Phonics They Use* (Cunningham, 2000), are bursting with engaging ideas. What follows is a sampling of activities that have proven to be effective.

Alphabet Scrapbook (Bear, Invernizzi, Templeton, & Johnston, 2000)

Prepare a blank dictionary for each child by stapling together sheets of paper. (Seven sheets of paper folded and stapled in the middle is enough for one letter per page.) Children can use this book in a variety of ways.

1. Practice writing uppercase and lowercase forms of the letter on each page.

2. Cut out letters in different fonts or styles from magazines and newspapers and paste them into their scrapbooks.

3. Draw and label pictures and other things which begin with that letter-sound.

4. Cut and paste magazine pictures onto the corresponding letter page. These pictures, too, can be labeled.

5. Add sight words as they become known, to create a personal dictionary.

Making Words (adapted from Cunningham, 2000)

In Making Words, students manipulate a group of letters to create words of varying lengths. They may create the words based on clues or simply list as many words as possible. Then they guess the mystery word—the source of the random letters. When creating the words, students may manipulate plastic letters or arrange magnetic letters on a cookie sheet.

Making and Writing Words (Rasinski, 1999a)

In this adaptation of Making Words, students follow the same procedure as in Making Words, but instead of manipulating the letters, students write them. An adaptation is to encourage students to manipulate the letters and then record them on the Making and Writing Words chart provided in the Rasinski article.

© McLaughlin & Fisher. (2005). *Research-Based Reading Lessons for K–3.* New York: Scholastic.

Making and Writing Words Using Letter Patterns (Rasinski, 1999b)

In this adaptation of Making and Writing Words, students use rimes (word families) and other patterns as well as individual letters to write words. (Rasinski's article provides the organizer.) Then the students transfer their knowledge to create new words. Finally, they cut up the organizer to create word cards, which they can use to practice the words in games and sorts.

Portable Word Walls (McLaughlin, 2003)

To use the word wall as a resource for students' reading and writing in class, for pull-out instructional situations, and at home, have the students create Portable Word Walls that they can take with them. This is easily accomplished by using manila folders and markers. For more information about word walls, see Appendix D.

Ideas for Creating Word Walls

- A word wall is a systematically organized collection of words that is displayed in large letters on a wall or other easily seen area in the classroom.

- A word wall is a tool for students that helps support the teaching of important general principles about words and how they work.

- Word wall lists vary. High-frequency words, onsets and rimes, and help lists are three examples.

- Word walls provide support for students, help them to remember connections between words, and promote independence during their reading and writing.

- New words should be added gradually and should be easily viewed by all students.

- Writing in large black letters on various background colors helps point out distinctions between words.

- Practicing words through various chants, games, conversations, and writing activities helps students to take ownership of words and naturally use them in their everyday language.

Help Walls

A Help Wall is a display of words, ideas, or areas of studies for students to use to help them with their reading and writing. Your Help Wall should be unique to your classroom and to what the students have learned. Contractions, commonly misspelled words, editor's marks, synonyms and antonyms, homophones, punctuation rules, other words for "said," parts of speech, verb tenses, prepositions, vowel sounds, prefixes and suffixes, and capitalization rules are examples of items that may be included. Students may also create their own Portable Help Walls to add to throughout the year. Students often take these Portable Help Walls home.

© McLaughlin & Fisher. (2005). Research-Based Reading Lessons for K–3. New York: Scholastic.

Ideas to include on Help Walls:

CONTRACTIONS	COMPOUND WORDS	OTHER WORDS FOR "SAID"	SYNONYMS
I've	cupcake	told	big – large
you've	teacup	explained	small – tiny
I'd	butterfly	responded	fast – quick
you'd	basketball	shouted	sick – ill
she'd	bookcase	replied	laugh – giggle
he'd	wastebasket	exclaimed	throw – toss
aren't	shoelace	proclaimed	enjoy – like
shouldn't	backpack	whispered	stole – took
haven't	toothpaste	commented	present – gift
wouldn't		remarked	

ANTONYMS	HOMOPHONES	COMMONLY MISSPELLED WORDS	
hot – cold	blue – blew	a lot	
on – off	there – their	weird	
dark – light	to – too – two	all right	
in – out	here – hear	occasion	
up – down	no – know	receive	
stop – go	write – right	separate	

VOWEL SOUNDS

Short *a* – apple	Long *a* – ape
Short *e* – exercise	Long *e* – eat
Short *i* – itch	Long *i* – ice
Short *o* – octopus	Long *o* – open
Short *u* – umbrella	Long *u* – unicorn

PUNCTUATION USAGE

period (.)	Please stop tapping your pencil.
question mark (?)	What time is it?
exclamation mark (!)	You did a great job!

Onsets and Rimes

RIMES					
-ack	-an	-aw	-ick	-ing	-op
-unk	-ain	-ank	-ay	-ide	-ink
-or	-ake	-ap	-eat	-ight	-ip
-ore	-ale	-ash	-ell	-ill	-ir
-uck	-all	-at	-est	-in	-ock
-ug	-ame	-ate	-ice	-ine	-oke
-ump					

ONSETS AND RIMES					
back	man	saw	sick	sing	hop
dunk	main	tank	way	side	sink
for	make	tap	beat	light	tip
more	sale	dash	tell	bill	stir
duck	tall	sat	west	chin	block
bug	same	late	mice	nine	joke
bump					

© McLaughlin & Fisher (2005). *Research-Based Reading Lessons for K–3*. New York: Scholastic.

High-Frequency Words

PREPRIMER		PRIMER		FIRST		SECOND		THIRD	
a	red	all	out	after	once	always	right	about	only
and	run	am	please	again	open	around	sing	better	out
away	said	are	pretty	an	over	because	sit	bring	own
big	see	at	ran	any	put	been	sleep	carry	pick
blue	the	ate	ride	as	round	before	tell	clean	seven
can	three	be	saw	ask	some	best	their	done	shall
come	to	black	say	by	stop	both	these	draw	show
down	two	brown	she	could	take	buy	those	drink	six
find	up	but	so	every	thank	call	upon	eight	small
for	we	came	soon	fly	them	cold	us	fall	start
funny	where	did	that	from	then	does	use	far	ten
go	yellow	do	there	give	think	don't	very	full	today
help	you	eat	they	going	walk	fast	wash	got	together
here		four	this	had	warm	first	which	grow	try
I		get	too	has	were	five	why	hold	
in		good	under	her	when	found	work	hot	
is		have	want	him		gave	would	hurt	
it		he	was	his		goes	write	if	
little		into	well	how		green	your	keep	
look		like	went	jump		its		kind	
make		must	what	know		made		laugh	
me		new	white	let		many		light	
my		no	who	live		off		long	
not		now	will	may		or		much	
one		on	with	of		pull		myself	
play		our	yes	old		read		never	

Ideas for Teaching Fluency

Fluent Reading Models

Providing fluent reading models for students helps them become fluent readers. Teachers, parents, cross-age volunteers, and books on tape can all be good fluency models for students. (See Chapter 4, Lesson 1, p. 83.)

Echo Reading

In echo reading, the teacher reads a line of poetry or a sentence from a story, and the students "echo" the teacher's fluent reading. This technique affords students interaction with a fluent model and helps them to notice aspects of fluency, such as the teacher's phrasing, expression, and use of punctuation. Echo reading encourages students to read fluently when they engage with text independently. (See Chapter 4, Lesson 2, p. 88.)

Choral Reading

In choral reading, the teacher and the students read together. When engaging in choral reading, the pressure is off the individual reader, so there is more of a tendency to focus on the fluent manner in which the poem or text segment is being read. (See Chapter 4, Lesson 3, p. 91.)

Repeated Readings

Repeated readings of a text help students read it more fluently. The process "consists of reading a short, meaningful passage several times until a satisfactory level of fluency is reached. Then the procedure is practiced with a new passage" (Samuels, 1979, p. 376). This improves comprehension because as the reading becomes more fluent, less emphasis is placed on decoding and more on comprehension. (See Chapter 4, Lesson 4, p. 94, for an adaptation of Samuels' Repeated Readings.)

Readers Theater

Readers Theater is like a read-through of a script. A narrator often introduces the work, sets the scene, and provides transitional information during the performance. The readers use their voices to create the scene and bring the characters to life. Books that have a lot of dialogue can be used for Readers Theater. A number of Web sites also provide scripts for this technique. (See Chapter 4, Lesson 5, p. 97.)

© McLaughlin & Fisher. (2005). *Research-Based Reading Lessons for K–3*. New York: Scholastic.

Appendix F

Comprehension Strategies, Teaching Ideas, and Blacklines

STRATEGY	TEACHING IDEA	PAGE	BLACKLINE
Previewing	Story Impressions	190	203
Self-Questioning	"I Wonder" Statements	191	204
Making Connections	Drawing Connections	192	205
Visualizing	Draw and Label Visualizations	193	206
Knowing How Words Work	Concept of Definition Map	194	207
	Semantic Map	195	208
	Semantic Question Map	196	209
	Synonym Rhymes	197	210
	Vocabulary Bookmark Technique	198	211
Monitoring	Bookmark Technique	199	212-213
Summarizing	Draw and Label Retelling	200	214
Evaluating	Discussion Web	201	215
	Comparison/Contrast Charts	202	216

(TEACHING IDEA) Story Impressions

Comprehension Strategies: Previewing, Making Connections

(See blackline, p. 203)

TEXT: Narrative

USE: Before reading, to introduce story vocabulary, make predictions, and make connections to the story structure

PROCEDURE:

1. Explain previewing and Story Impressions.

2. Think aloud while demonstrating writing a Story Impression.

3. Provide students with a list of words that provide clues about the story. Choose words that relate to the narrative elements—characters, setting, problem, events, and solution. Limit the list to ten words, using no more than five words per clue. Present the clues in a list in the order in which they appear in the story. Connect them with downward arrows.

4. Have students read the list of words in order and work in small groups to write a Story Impression, using the words in the order in which they were presented.

5. Have each group share its Story Impression with the class. Discuss each story.

6. Read the original story to the class and engage students in a discussion of comparisons and contrasts.

7. For variety, adapt this technique to Poem Impressions using story poems or Picture Impressions, in which the students sketch in response to the clues provided.

8. When using this technique with very young students, share a short list of clues, develop a Story Impression orally with the whole class, and record the story on a posterboard, the chalkboard, or an overhead transparency.

EXAMPLE LESSON: Chapter 6, p. 140

SOURCE: McGinley, W. & Denner, P. (1987). Story impressions: A prereading/prewriting activity. *Journal of Reading, 31*, 248–253.

© McLaughlin & Fisher (2005). *Research-Based Reading Lessons for K–3.* New York: Scholastic.

(TEACHING IDEA) "I Wonder" Statements

Comprehension Strategies: Previewing, Self-Questioning

(See blackline, p. 204)

TEXT: Narrative, Expository

USE: Before and during reading to promote Self-Questioning and active thinking

PROCEDURE:

1. Explain Self-Questioning and how to create "I Wonder" Statements and support them with reasoning; provide prompts such as "I wonder . . . because . . ."

2. Think aloud while demonstrating how to wonder orally, in writing, and by sketching.

3. Guide students to wonder about things in everyday life, stories, or ideas presented in texts.

4. Share wonders and discuss with text support, if possible.

5. Encourage students to wonder throughout the reading of a text.

EXAMPLE LESSON: Chapter 6, p. 146

SOURCE: Harvey, S., & Goudvis, A. (2000). *Strategies that work*. York, ME: Stenhouse.

(TEACHING IDEA) Drawing Connections

Comprehension Strategy: Making Connections (See blackline, p.205)

TEXT: Narrative, Expository

USE: During and after reading to provide a structure to create visual representations to make text-text, text-self, and text-world connections

PROCEDURE:

1. Explain how to make connections.

2. Think aloud while demonstrating how to use visual representations (pictures, shapes, lines) to communicate connections to text, self, or world.

3. Make a connection and model writing one or more sentences about the connection.

4. Have students listen to a selection and then ask them to create a visual representation of their connection and write a sentence about it. Ask them to share their drawings in small groups, explaining the connections they made.

5. Encourage students to draw connections for a text they are reading on their own. Have them write a sentence or paragraph explaining their connection.

EXAMPLE LESSON: Chapter 6, p. 151

SOURCE: McLaughlin, M., & Allen, M. B. (2002). *Guided comprehension: A teaching model for grades 3–8.* Newark, DE: International Reading Association.

© McLaughlin & Fisher. (2005). *Research-Based Reading Lessons for K–3.* New York: Scholastic.

(TEACHING IDEA) Draw and Label Visualizations

Comprehension Strategy: Visualizing (See blackline, p. 206)

TEXT: Narrative, Expository

USE: During and after reading, to visually represent and label mental images created while reading

PROCEDURE:

1. Explain visualizing and how to visualize (create mental pictures while reading).

2. Demonstrate how to use visual representations (pictures, shapes, lines) to communicate mental pictures.

3. Think aloud about what you see in your mind and how you will express it in a drawing. Then think aloud about what you will write to label the drawing (one or more sentences).

4. Have students listen to a selection and then ask them to create a visual representation of their mind pictures and write about it. Ask them to share their drawings in pairs or small groups and explain the images they saw in their minds.

5. Encourage students to visualize while they read.

EXAMPLE LESSON: Chapter 6, p. 155

SOURCE: Adapted from McLaughlin, M., & Allen, M. B. (2002). *Guided comprehension: A teaching model for grades 3–8.* Newark, DE: International Reading Association.

(TEACHING IDEA) Concept of Definition Map

Comprehension Strategies: Knowing How Words Work, Summarizing (See blackline, p. 207)

TEXT: Expository

USE: Before and after reading, to build connections between background knowledge and new words; to summarize

PROCEDURE:

1. Explain knowing how words work and what a Concept of Definition Map tells us about words.

2. Think aloud while demonstrating how to complete a Concept Map.

3. Select, or have students select, a word to be defined, and write the word in the "Focus Word" oval.

4. Ask students to determine what broad category best describes the word in the "What is it?" section. Examples: Pizza is a food; a city is a place.

5. Ask students to provide a viable synonym for the section labeled "A comparison."

6. Ask students to provide some words that describe the focus word in the "How would you describe it?" section.

7. Ask students to provide some specific examples of the word in the "What are some examples?" section. These can be specific items or descriptions of examples.

8. If the map is complete, use it to create an oral or written summary. If the map is not complete, read a selection that will provide the missing information and complete the map after reading. Use the completed map to create an oral or written summary.

EXAMPLE LESSON: Chapter 5, p. 115

SOURCE: Schwartz, R. & Raphael, T. (1985). Concept of definition: A key to improving students' vocabulary. *The Reading Teacher, 39* (2), 198–205.

© McLaughlin & Fisher. (2005). *Research-Based Reading Lessons for K–3.* New York: Scholastic.

(TEACHING IDEA) Semantic Map

Comprehension Strategies: Knowing How Words Work,
Previewing, Summarizing (See blackline, p. 208)

TEXT: Narrative, Expository

USE: Before and after reading to gain an overview of a topic, make predictions about
text, introduce vocabulary, and summarize information

PROCEDURE:

1. Choose a focus word related to the text and write it in the center oval of the
Semantic Map graphic on the board or overhead projector.

2. Explain knowing how words work and Semantic Maps.

3. Introduce the focus word and discuss.

4. Think aloud while demonstrating how to complete the map.

5. Begin by brainstorming a few words that come to mind when you think about the
focus word. Then invite the students to contribute words they associate with the
focus word.

6. Record (or have students record) responses on the board.

7. After brainstorming, examine the list of related words to see what categories
emerge.

8. Record a category in each of the four remaining ovals and list related words
beneath each category.

9. After reading, revisit the map to revise, add, or delete information as necessary.

10. Use the completed Semantic Map to create an oral or written summary.

EXAMPLE LESSON: Chapter 5, p. 109

SOURCE: Johnson, D. D., & Pearson, P. D. (1984). *Teaching reading vocabulary* (2nd ed.).
New York: Holt, Rinehart, and Winston.

(TEACHING IDEA) Semantic Question Map

Comprehension Strategies: Knowing How Words Work,
Previewing, Summarizing (See blackline, p. 209)

TEXT: Narrative, Expository

USE: Before and after reading, to gain an overview of a topic and make predictions about text

PROCEDURE:

1. Choose a focus word from the text, develop four related questions, and write them on the Semantic Question Map blackline.

2. Explain knowing how words work and Semantic Question Maps.

3. Introduce the focus word and discuss.

4. Think aloud while demonstrating how to complete the map.

5. Invite students to respond to each question.

6. Record (or have students record) responses directly below each question.

7. Discuss the information on the map.

8. Read (or have students read) a text that will contribute information to the map.

9. Revisit the map to revise, add, or delete information as necessary.

10. Use the completed Semantic Question Map to create an oral or written summary.

EXAMPLE LESSON: Chapter 5, p. 125

SOURCE: Adapted from Johnson, D. D., & Pearson, P. D. (1984). *Teaching reading vocabulary* (2nd ed.). New York: Holt, Rinehart, and Winston.

© McLaughlin & Fisher. (2005). *Research-Based Reading Lessons for K–3.* New York: Scholastic.

(TEACHING IDEA) Synonym Rhymes

Comprehension Strategy: Knowing How Words Work

(See blackline, p. 210)

TEXT: Narrative

USE: Before reading, to learn how synonyms work and write alternative versions of rhymes

PROCEDURE:

1. Explain knowing how words work and Synonym Rhymes.

2. Think aloud while demonstrating how to use synonyms in nursery rhymes and short poems.

3. Share original rhymes or poems. Discuss and use these as the models for Synonym Rhymes.

4. Share the rhyme or poem with one word deleted from each line.

5. Brainstorm (or have pairs of students brainstorm) synonyms to replace the deleted words. Use dictionaries or student thesauruses to help find synonyms to replace the words that have been deleted.

6. Share new rhymes, poems.

7. Use the structure of the original poem to create new poems or rewrite nursery rhymes with new characters or events.

EXAMPLE LESSON: Chapter 5, p. 121

SOURCE: Adapted from McLaughlin, M., & Allen, M. B. (2002). *Guided comprehension in action: Lessons for grades 3–8.* Newark, DE: International Reading Association.

(TEACHING IDEA) Vocabulary Bookmark Technique

Comprehension Strategies: Monitoring, Knowing How Words Work

(See blackline, p. 211)

TEXT: Narrative, Expository

USE: During reading, to monitor comprehension, learn vocabulary, and understand how words work

PROCEDURE:

1. Explain Vocabulary Bookmark Technique. Explain that during reading students will each choose a vocabulary word that they think the whole class needs to talk about. They will record (write or sketch) the word and what they think it means on the Vocabulary Bookmark blackline. They will also write the page number and the number of the paragraph where their word choice is located.

2. Think aloud while demonstrating how to use Vocabulary Bookmark Technique.

3. Invite the students to complete Vocabulary Bookmarks.

4. Use completed bookmarks as the basis of discussion. Have students explain what their words mean and how to use them. Revisit the text to locate words and check their meanings in context. Use dictionaries to verify the words' meanings, if necessary.

5. Add selected words to the class word wall, and encourage students to use the words in their speaking and writing vocabularies.

EXAMPLE LESSON: Chapter 5, p. 130

SOURCE: McLaughlin, M. (2003). *Guided comprehension in the Primary Grades*. Newark, DE: International Reading Association.

© McLaughlin & Fisher. (2005). *Research-Based Reading Lessons for K–3.* New York: Scholastic.

(TEACHING IDEA) Bookmark Technique

Comprehension Strategies: Monitoring, Knowing How Words Work

(See blacklines, p. 212–213)

TEXT: Narrative, Expository

USE: During reading, to monitor comprehension and understand how words work

PROCEDURE:

1. Explain monitoring and Bookmark Technique. Explain that there are four bookmarks. As students read, they make decisions and record (write or sketch) information on each bookmark. This includes the page and paragraph where their choice is located and the following specific information for each bookmark:

   Bookmark 1: Write or sketch the part of the text that is most interesting.

   Bookmark 2: Write or sketch the part of the text that is confusing.

   Bookmark 3: Write a word the whole class needs to discuss; provide a possible meaning.

   Bookmark 4: Write about an illustration, map, chart, or graph that helped you understand the text.

2. Think aloud while demonstrating how to use Bookmark Technique.

3. Invite the students to complete bookmarks.

4. Use completed bookmarks as the basis of discussion.

EXAMPLE LESSON: Chapter 6, p. 161

SOURCE: McLaughlin, M., & Allen, M. B. (2002). *Guided comprehension: A teaching model for grades 3–8.* Newark, DE: International Reading Association.

(TEACHING IDEA) Draw and Label Retelling

Comprehension Strategy: Summarizing (See blackline, p. 214)

TEXT: Narrative

USE: After reading, to recount the narrative elements and summarize

PROCEDURE:

1. Explain summarizing and the Draw and Label Retelling (Who? Where? What happened? How did the story end?).

2. Think aloud while demonstrating how to complete a Draw and Label Retelling.

3. Introduce a story, read it aloud, and discuss it.

4. Demonstrate simple lines and shapes that can be used to draw the retelling.

5. Remind students that we write labels in complete sentences.

6. Draw and label two sections of the retelling and ask the students to work with partners to complete the remaining sections.

7. Use the completed Draw and Label Retelling to orally summarize the story.

8. Invite the students to read a story in small groups and provide support as each group completes its Draw and Label Retelling. (You may want to give each student in the group a card listing a specific story element, for example, Who?: characters; Where?: setting; What happened?: problem and attempts to resolve the problem; How did it end?: resolution.)

9. Discuss the retellings and encourage students to retell stories they read.

EXAMPLE LESSON: Chapter 6, p. 165

SOURCE: Adapted from Morrow, L. M. (1985). Retelling stories: A strategy for improving children's comprehension, concept of story, and oral language complexity. *Elementary School Journal, 85* (5), 647–661.

© McLaughlin & Fisher (2005). *Research-Based Reading Lessons for K–3.* New York: Scholastic.

(TEACHING IDEA) Discussion Web

Comprehension Strategy: Evaluating (See blackline, p. 215)

TEXT: Expository

USE: During and after reading, to make judgments about the author's purpose and to determine perspectives

PROCEDURE:

1. Chose a topic or question that has two different perspectives (pro and con) and find readings to support both sides of the issue.

2. Explain evaluating and how to use a Discussion Web.

3. Think aloud while demonstrating how to use a Discussion Web.

4. Write the focus question in the space provided on the blackline.

5. Read a text that supports the issue and one that doesn't.

6. Record a few ideas that support the issue/question in the Yes column.

7. Record a few ideas that take the opposite perspective in the No column.

8. Think aloud about your placement of the ideas.

9. Invite pairs of students to suggest text-based ideas to record in each column.

10. Discuss the question and supporting ideas with the students. Invite them to draw conclusions in small groups or pairs and write them and their reasons in the space provided on the blackline.

11. Discuss the conclusions and reasons as a class and come to a consensus.

12. Record the class's conclusion and rationale on the Discussion Web used for demonstration.

EXAMPLE LESSON: Chapter 6, p. 170

SOURCE: Alvermann, D. (1991). The discussion web: A graphic aid for learning across the curriculum. *The Reading Teacher, 45,* 92–99.

(TEACHING IDEA) Comparison/Contrast Charts

Comprehension Strategy: Evaluating (See blackline, p. 216)

TEXT: Narrative, Expository

USE: After reading, to note similarities and differences between texts, topics, characters, or illustrations

PROCEDURE:

1. Explain evaluating and how to use Comparison/Contrast Charts.

2. Think aloud while demonstrating how Comparison/Contrast Charts work.

3. Read a text aloud to the students.

4. After reading, discuss two characters or illustrations that have similarities and differences. Explain that similarities are comparisons and differences are contrasts.

5. Record similarities in the "Comparisons" column; record differences in the "Contrasts" column. Use specific words, phrases, or events from the text to support ideas.

6. Discuss the comparisons and contrasts with the students.

7. Encourage the students to look for similarities and differences in texts, topics, characters, and illustrations while reading.

EXAMPLE USE: In Chapter 6, Lesson 1, a Comparison/Contrast Chart is used to show similarities and differences between students' Story Impressions and the original story.

SOURCE: Adapted from Tompkins, G. (2001). *Literacy for the 21st century: A balanced approach* (2nd ed.). Saddle Brook, NJ: Prentice Hall.

© McLaughlin & Fisher. (2005). *Research-Based Reading Lessons for K–3.* New York: Scholastic.

Story Impression

Names _____

Clues

Title: _____

Name_____

I Wonder Bookmark

Page_____

I wonder _____

_____

_____

because _____

_____

Page_____

I wonder _____

_____

_____

because _____

_____

Name _____

Drawing Connections

Drawing: Sketch your connection.

Label: Write a sentence to explain your drawing.

_____

_____

_____

Name _____

Draw and Label Visualizations

Drawing: Sketch your visualization.

Label: Write a sentence to explain your drawing.

_____

_____

Name _____

Concept of Definition Map

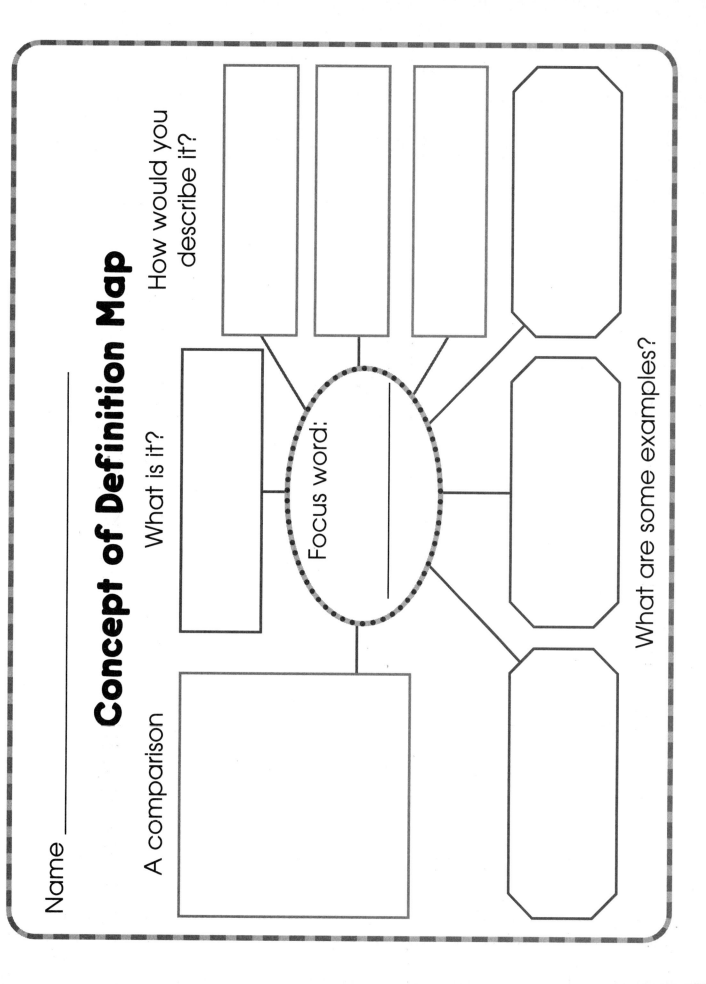

What is it?

How would you describe it?

A comparison

Focus word: _____

What are some examples?

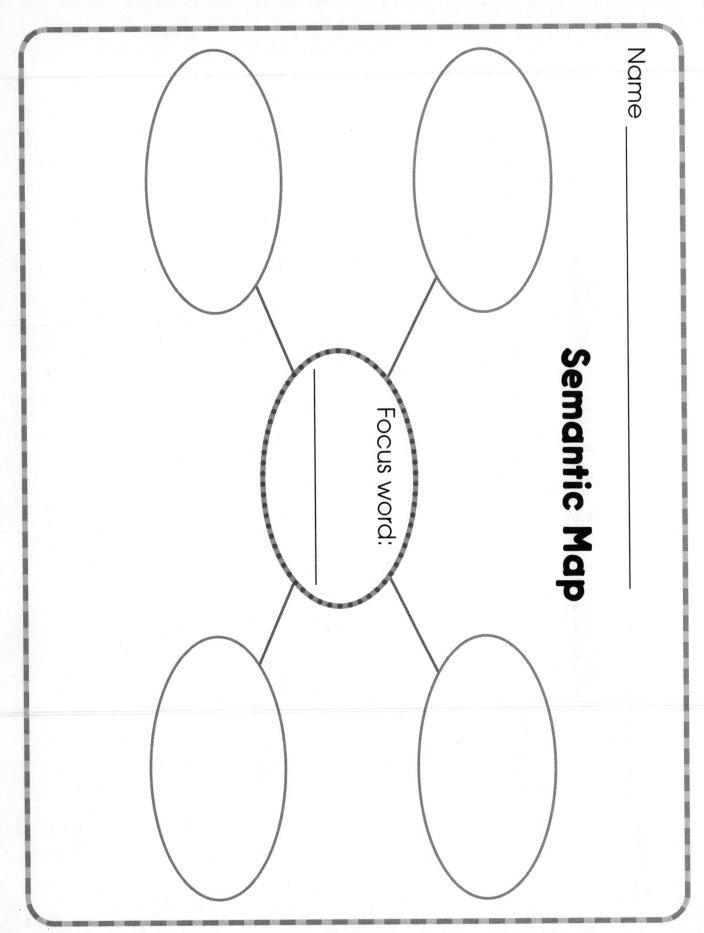

Name _____

Semantic Map

Focus word: _____

Name _____

Semantic Question Map

Question 1:

Question 2:

Focus word:
_____

Question 3:

Question 4:

Name_____

Synonym Rhymes

Part One: Replace each missing word with a synonym.

Jack and Jill _____ up the hill

To _____ a pail of water.

Jack fell down and broke his _____

And Jill came _____ after.

Part Two: Write a silly version of a rhyme using the same structure.

_____

_____

_____

_____

Name_____

Vocabulary
Bookmark

A word I think the
whole class needs to
talk about is . . .

Page_____

Paragraph_____

Name_____

Bookmark One

The most interesting part was . . .

Page_____

Paragraph_____

Name_____

Bookmark Two

Something that confused me was . . .

Page_____

Paragraph_____

Name_____

Bookmark Three

A word I think the whole class needs to talk about is . . .

Page_____

Paragraph_____

Name_____

Bookmark Four

The illustration, chart, map, or graph that helped me understand what I was reading was . . .

Page_____

Paragraph_____

Name _____

Draw and Label Retelling

Who?
Draw:

Label: _____

Where?
Draw:

Label: _____

What happened?
Draw:

Label: _____

How did it end?
Draw:

Label: _____

Discussion Web

Name _____

Yes

No

Reasons

Discussion Topic/Question

Conclusion

Reason

Comparison/Contrast Chart

Comparisons

1. _____

2. _____

3. _____

4. _____

5. _____

Contrasts

1. _____

2. _____

3. _____

4. _____

5. _____

© McLaughlin & Fisher. (2005). Research-Based Reading Lessons for K–3. New York: Scholastic. Page 216

Center Planner and Student Self-Assessment

Center Planner

Center: _____

Theme: _____

Skill or strategy focus: _____

Format: ❑ Display Board ❑ Box ❑ Other (_____)

Accountability:

Assessment: ❑ Review skill/strategy applications

❑ Student self-assessments

Record-keeping: ❑ Reading portfolios

❑ Center folders

❑ Other (_____)

Materials needed: _____

_____

Sample teaching idea: _____

Adapted from McLaughlin, M. (2003). *Guided comprehension in the primary grades.* Newark, DE: International Reading Association.

My Center and Routine Assessment

Name _____

Date _____

1. I used my time wisely.	**1**	**2**	**3**	**4**	**5**
2. I followed the directions carefully.	**1**	**2**	**3**	**4**	**5**
3. I finished all my work.	**1**	**2**	**3**	**4**	**5**
4. I worked well with my partners.	**1**	**2**	**3**	**4**	**5**
5. Overall, I give myself a	**1**	**2**	**3**	**4**	**5**

Next time, I will _____

_____

_____

My teacher thinks _____

_____

_____

© McLaughlin & Fisher. (2005). *Research-Based Reading Lessons for K–3.* New York: Scholastic. Page 218

References

Alvermann, D. (1991). The discussion web: A graphic aid for learning across the curriculum. *The Reading Teacher, 45*, 92-99.

Anderson, R. C. (1994). Role of reader's schema in comprehension, learning, and memory. In R. B. Ruddell, M. R. Ruddell, & H. Singer (Eds.), *Theoretical models and processes of reading* (4th ed., pp. 469–482). Newark, DE: International Reading Association.

Anderson, R. C. & Pearson, P. D. (1984). A schema-theoretic view of basic processes in reading comprehension. In P. D. Pearson, R. Barr, M. L. Kamil, & P. Mosenthal (Eds.), *Handbook of reading research* (Vol. 1, pp. 225–253). New York: Longman.

Askew, B. J. & Fountas, I. (1998). Building an early reading process: Active from the start! *The Reading Teacher, 52* (2), 126–134.

Asselin, M. (2002). Vocabulary instruction. *Teacher Librarian, 29* (3), 57–59.

Ball, E. & Blachman, B. (1991). Does phoneme awareness training in kindergarten make a difference in early word recognition and developmental spelling? *Reading Research Quarterly, 26*, 49-66.

Bear, D. R., Invernizzi, M., Templeton, S., & Johnston, F. (2003). *Words their way: Word study for phonics, vocabulary, and spelling.* (3rd ed.). Upper Saddle River, NJ: Merrill. (Videotape: Words their way video, ISBN: 013022183X)

Blachowicz, C. L., & Fisher, P. (2000). Vocabulary instruction. In M. L. Kamil, P. Mosenthal, P. D. Pearson, & R. Barr (Eds.), *Handbook of reading research* (Vol. 3, pp. 503–523). Mahwah, NJ: Erlbaum.

Buehl, D. (2001). *Classroom strategies for interactive learning* (2nd ed.). Newark, DE: International Reading Association.

Cambourne, B. (2002). Holistic, integrated approaches to reading and language arts instruction: The constructivist framework of an instructional theory. In A. Farstrup & J. Samuels (Eds.), *What research has to say about reading instruction* (3rd ed., pp. 25–47). Newark, DE: International Reading Association.

Cunningham, P. (2000). *Phonics they use: Words for reading and writing* (3rd ed.). New York: HarperCollins.

Duke, N., & Pearson, P. D. (2002). Effective practices for developing comprehension. In A. Farstrup & J. Samuels (Eds.), *What research has to say about reading instruction* (3rd ed., pp. 205–242). Newark, DE: International Reading Association.

Ehri, L. C., & Nunes, S. R. (2002). The role of phonemic awareness in learning to read. In A. Farstrup & S. Samuels (Eds.), *What research has to say about reading instruction* (3rd ed., pp. 110–139). Newark, DE: International Reading Association.

Farstrup, A. & Samuels, J. (Eds.). (2002). *What research has to say about reading instruction.* Newark, DE: International Reading Association.

Fountas, I. C. & Pinnell, G. S. (1999). *Matching books to readers: Using leveled books in guided reading, K–3.* Portsmouth, NH: Heinemann.

Fredericks, A. (2001). *The complete phonemic awareness handbook.* Orlando, FL: Rigby Press.

Gambrell, L. B. (1996). Creating classroom cultures that foster reading motivation. *The Reading Teacher, 50* (1), 14–25.

Graves, M., & Watts–Taffe, S. (2002). The place of word consciousness in a research-based vocabulary program. In A. Farstrup & S. Samuels (Eds.). *What research has to say about reading instruction.* (3rd ed., pp. 140–165). Newark, DE: International Reading Association.

Guthrie, J. T. & Wigfield, A. (2000). Engagement and motivation in reading. In M. L. Kamil, P. Mosenthal, P. D. Pearson, & R. Barr (Eds.) *Handbook of reading research* (Vol. 3, pp. 403–422). Mahwah, NJ: Erlbaum.

Harris, T. L., & Hodges, R. E. (Eds.). (1995). *The literacy dictionary: The vocabulary of reading and writing.* Newark, DE: International Reading Association.

Harvey, S. & Goudvis, A. (2000). *Strategies that work: Teaching comprehension to enhance understanding.* York, ME: Stenhouse.

Hilden, K. & Pressley, M. (2002). *Can teachers become comprehension strategy teachers given a small amount of training?* Paper presented at the 52nd Annual Meeting of the National Reading Conference, Miami, FL.

International Reading Association. (1998). *Phonemic awareness and the teaching of reading: A position statement of the International Reading Association.* Newark, DE: International Reading Association.

International Reading Association. (2000). *Excellent reading teachers: A position statement of the International Reading Association.* Newark, DE: International Reading Association.

International Reading Association. (2002). *IRA Literacy Study Groups vocabulary module.* Newark, DE: International Reading Association.

Johnson, D. D. & Pearson, P. D. (1984). *Teaching reading vocabulary* (2nd ed.). New York: Holt, Rinehart, Winston.

Kamil, M., Pearson, P. D. & Barr, R. (Eds.). (2000). *Handbook of Reading Research* (Vol. 3). Mahwah, NJ: Erlbaum.

McGinley, W. & Denner, P. (1987). Story impressions: A prereading/prewriting activity. *Journal of Reading, 31,* 248-253.

McLaughlin, M. (2003). *Guided comprehension in the primary grades.* Newark, DE: International Reading Association.

McLaughlin, M. & Allen, M. B. (2002a). *Guided comprehension: A teaching model for grades 3–8.* Newark, DE: International Reading Association.

McLaughlin, M. & Allen, M. B. (2002b). *Guided comprehension in action: Lessons for grades 3–8.* Newark, DE: International Reading Association.

Morrow, L. M. (1985). Retelling stories: A strategy for improving children's comprehension, concept of story, and oral language complexity. *Elementary School Journal, 85* (5), 647-661.

Nathan, R. & Stanovich, K. (1991). The causes and consequences of differences in reading fluency. *Theory into Practice, 30,* 176-184.

National Commission on Teaching and America's Future. (1997). *Doing what matters most: Investing in quality teaching.* Available at http://www.tc.columbia.edu/teachingcomm.

National Reading Panel. (2000). *Teaching children to read: An evidence-based assessment of the scientific research literature on reading and its implications for reading instruction.* Washington, DC: National Institutes of Health.

Oakley, G. (2003). Improving oral reading fluency (and comprehension) through the creation of talking books. *Reading Online, 6*(7). Retrieved from http://readingonline.org/articles/oakley.

Pearson, P. D. (2001). *Comprehension strategy instruction: An idea whose time has come again.* Paper presented at the Annual Meeting of the Colorado Council of the International Reading Association, Denver, CO.

Pressley, M. (2000). What should comprehension instruction be the instruction of? In M. Kamil, P. Mosenthal, P. D. Pearson, & R. Barr (Eds.), *Handbook of reading research* (Vol. 3, pp. 545–561). Mahwah, NJ: Erlbaum.

Rasinski, T. V. (1999a). Making and writing words. *Reading Online,* an electronic journal of the International Reading Association. Available at http://www.readingonline.org/articles/words/rasinski.index.html.

Rasinski, T. V. (1999b). Making and writing words using letter patterns. *Reading Online,* an electronic journal of the International Reading Association. Available at http://www.readingonline.org/articles/words/rasinski_index.html.

Rasinski, T. V. (2003). *The fluent reader.* New York: Scholastic.

Rasinski, T. V. (2004). Creating fluent readers. *Educational Leadership, 61* (6), 46–51.

Rasinski, T. V., & Padak, N. (2000). *Effective reading strategies: Children who find reading difficult.* (2nd ed.). Columbus, OH: Merrill/Prentice Hall.

Richards, M. (2000). Be a good detective: Solve the case of oral reading fluency. *The Reading Teacher, 53* (7), 534–539.

Ruddell, R. B. (2004). Researching the influential literacy teacher: Characteristics, beliefs, strategies, and new research directions. In R. B. Ruddell & N. J. Unrau (Eds.), *Theoretical models and processes of reading* (5th ed., pp. 979–997). Newark, DE: International Reading Association.

Samuels, S. J. (1979). The method of repeated readings. *The Reading Teacher, 32,* 403–408.

Samuels, S. J. (2002). Reading fluency: Its development and assessment. In A. Farstrup & S. Samuels (Eds.), *What research has to say about reading* (3rd ed., pp.166–183). Newark, DE: International Reading Association.

© McLaughlin & Fisher. (2005). *Research-Based Reading Lessons for K–3.* New York: Scholastic.

Schwartz, R., & Raphael, T. (1985). Concept of definition: A key to improving students' vocabulary. *The Reading Teacher, 39*, 198–205.

Snow, C. E., Burns, M. S., & Griffin, P. G. (Eds.) (1998). *Preventing reading difficulties in young children*. Washington, DC: National Academy Press.

Stahl, S. A. (1992). Saying the "p" word: Nine guidelines for exemplary phonics instruction. *The Reading Teacher, 45* (8), 618–625.

Stahl, S. A., Duffy-Hester, A. M., & Stahl, K. A. D. (1998). Theory and research in practice: Everything you wanted to know about phonics (but were afraid to ask). *Reading Research Quarterly, 33* (3), 338–355.

Tompkins, G. (2001). *Literacy for the 21st century: A balanced approach* (2nd ed.). Saddle Brook, NJ: Prentice Hall.

Yopp, H. K. (1992). Developing phonemic awareness in young children. *The Reading Teacher, 45* (9), 696–703.

Yopp, H. K. (1995). Read-aloud books for developing phonemic awareness. *The Reading Teacher, 48* (6), 538–542.

Yopp, H. K. (1988). The validity and reliability of phonemic awareness tests. *Reading Research Quarterly, 23* (2), 159–177.

Yopp, H. K., & Yopp, R. H. (2000). Supporting phonemic awareness development in the in the classroom. *The Reading Teacher, 54*, 130–143.

Children's Books

Adler, D. A. (2003). *Mama played baseball*. New York: Harcourt Brace.

Ahlberg, J. & Ahlberg, A. (1978). *Each peach pear plum*. New York: Viking.

Andreae, G. (2002). *K is for kissing a cool kangaroo*. New York: Orchard Books.

Axtell, D. (1999). *We're going on a lion hunt*. New York: Henry Holt.

Bartoletti, S. C. (1996). *Growing up in coal country*. Boston: Houghton Mifflin.

Beaumont, K. (2004). *Duck, duck, goose! (A coyote's on the loose!)*. New York: HarperCollins.

Blackwell, D. (1989). *An ABC bestiary*. New York: Farrar, Straus, Giroux.

Bloom, B. (1999). *Wolf!* New York: Orchard Books.

Brown, K. (2001). *What's the time, Grandma Wolf?* Atlanta: Peachtree.

Brown, M. (1996). *Arthur's reading race*. New York: Random House.

Brown, M. (1996). *Arthur writes a story*. New York: Little, Brown.

Busby, P. (2002). *First to fly: How Wilbur and Orville Wright invented the airplane*. New York: Crown Publishers.

Carle, E. (1989). *Eric Carle's animals, animals*. New York: Philomel.

Carle, E. (1989). *The very busy spider*. New York: Putnam.

Carle, E. (1991). *Pancakes, pancakes!* New York: Simon & Schuster.

Carle, E. (1981). *The very hungry caterpillar*. New York: Penguin.

Carle, E. (1997). *The secret birthday message*. New York: HarperCollins.

Carle, E. (1999). *The grouchy ladybug*. New York: HarperCollins.

Carle, E. (1999). *The very lonely firefly*. New York: Philomel.

Carle, E. (2000). *Does a kangaro have a mother too?* New York: HarperCollins.

Catalanotto, P. (2002). *Matthew A.B.C.* New York: Simon and Schuster.

Cherry, L. (1990). *The great kapok tree*. New York: Harcourt Brace.

Cowley, J. (2003). *Mrs. Wishy-Washy's farm*. New York: Philomel Books.

Cronin, D. (2000). *Click, clack, moo: Cows that type*. New York: Scholastic.

Cronin, D. (2002). *Giggle, giggle, quack*. New York: Scholastic.

Cronin, D. (2004). *Duck for president*. New York: Simon & Schuster Children's Publishing Division.

Day, A. (1993). *Carl's Masquerade*. New York: Farrar, Straus and Giroux.

Ehlert, L. (1982). *Eating the alphabet: Fruits and vegetables*. Harcourt Brace.

Fleming, D. (1994). *Barnyard banter*. New York: Henry Holt and Company.

Fowler, A. (1997). *Save the rain forests*. Danbury, CT: Children's Press.

Freedman, C. (2001). *Where's your smile, crocodile?* Atlanta, GA: Peachtree.

Gibbons, G. (1991). *Whales*. New York: Holiday House.

Gibbons, G. (1997). *Nature's green umbrella*. New York: Harpe Trophy.

Greene, R. G. (2004). *This is the teacher.* New York: Dutton Children's Books.

Griffiths, R. (2004). *Sharing a pizza.* Washington, DC: National Geographic.

Harris, J. (1999). *The three little dinosaurs.* Hong Kong: Pelican Publishing Company.

Herzog, B. (2004). *H is for home run.* Chelsea, MI: Sleeping Bear Press.

Jackson, E. (1994). *Cinder Edna.* New York: Lothrop, Lee & Shepard Books.

James, M. (2004). *At the farmer's market.* Washington, DC: National Geographic.

London, J. (1996). *Froggy goes to school.* Puffin Books.

Low, A. (2004). *Aunt Lucy went to buy a hat.* New York: HarperCollins.

Martin, B. (1970). *Brown bear, brown bear, what do you see?* New York: Henry Holt.

Martin, B. (1997). *Polar bear, polar bear, what do you hear?* New York: Henry Holt.

Martin, B. (2003). *Panda bear, panda bear, what do you see?* New York: Henry Holt.

Mitton, T. (2001). *Down by the cool of the pool.* New York: Orchard Books.

Nash, S. (2004). *TUFF FLUFF: The case of duckie's missing brain.* Cambridge, MA: Candlewick.

Numeroff, L. (1998). *If you give a pig a pancake.* New York: HarperCollins.

Numeroff, L. (2000). *If you take a mouse to the movies.* New York: HarperCollins.

Numeroff, L. (2002). *If you take a mouse to school.* New York: HarperCollins.

Palatini, M. (2001). *The Web files.* New York: Hyperion Books for Children.

Prelutsky, J. (1986). *Ride a purple pelican.* New York: Greenwillow Books.

Prelutsky, J. (1988). *Tyrannosaurus was a beast.* New York: Mulberry Books.

Prelutsky, J. (1986). *Read-aloud rhymes for the very young.* New York: Alfred A. Knopf.

Prelutsky, J. (1994). *A pizza the size of the sun.* New York: Greenwillow Books.

Pritchett, J. (2004). *Making pancakes.* Washington, DC: National Geographic.

Rappaport, D. (2001). *Martin's big words.* New York: Hyperion Books.

Sciezka, J. (1996). *The true story of the 3 little pigs!* New York: Puffin.

Scieszka, J. (1998). *Squids will be squids.* New York: Viking.

Scieszka, J. (2002). *The stinky cheese man and other fairly stupid tales.* New York: Viking.

Seuss, Dr. (1996). *Dr. Seuss's ABC: An amazing alphabet book!* New York: Random House.

Shaw, N. (1986). *Sheep in a jeep.* Boston: Houghton Mifflin.

Shulman, L. M. (2002). *Old MacDonald had a woodshop.* New York: Putnam.

Sierra, J. (2004). *Wild about books.* New York: Alfred A. Knopf.

Simon, S. (2000). *Gorillas.* New York: HarperCollins.

Simon, S. (1993). *Wolves.* New York: HarperCollins.

Slonim, D. (2003). *Oh, ducky.* San Francisco: Chronicle Books LLC.

Sturges, P. (1999). *The little red hen makes a pizza.* New York: Dutton.

Wildsmith, G. and Wildsmith, R. (1994). *Jack and the Meanstalk.* New York: Knopf.

Wilson, K. (2003). *Bear wants more.* New York: Margaret K. McElderry Books.

Yolen, J. (1993). *Welcome to the green house.* New York: Putnam.

Yolen, J. (2003). *My brothers' flying machine.* New York: Little Brown.

Index

A

ABC Bestiary, An, (Blackwell), 53
Adler, D. A., *Mama Played Baseball*, 170, 171
Ahlberg, J. & Ahlberg A., *Each Peach Pear Plum*, 31-32
Allen, M., 192, 193, 197, 198, 199
Alvermann, D., 201
Anderson, R. C., 137
Andreae, G., *K Is for Kissing a Cool Kangaroo*, 36
Arthur's Reading Race, (Brown), 148
Arthur Writes a Story, (Brown), 146-147
Askew, B. J., 12, 137
Asselin, M., 106
At the Farmer's Market, (James), 94
Aunt Lucy Went to Buy a Hat, (Low), 74
Axtell, D., *We're Going on a Lion Hunt*, 28-30

B

Ball, E., 15
Barnyard Banter, (Fleming), 42
Bartoletti, S., *Growing Up in Coal Country*, 173
Bear, D. et al., 79, 182
Bear Wants More, (Wilson), 70-72
Beaumont, K., *Duck, Duck, Goose! (A Coyote's on the Loose!)*, 36
Blachman, B., 15
Blachowicz, C.L., 107, 135
Blackwell, D., *ABC Bestiary, An*, 53
Bloom, B., *Wolf!*, 97-101
Brown, K., *What's the Time, Grandma Wolf?*, 101-103
Brown, M.
    Arthur's Reading Race, 148
    Arthur Writes a Story, 146-147
Brown Bear, Brown Bear, What Do You See?, (Martin), 23-24
Buehl, D., 135
Busby, P., *First to Fly*, 161

C

Cambourne, B., 137
Carle, E.
    Does a Kangaroo Have a Mother Too?, 47, 90
    Eric Carle's Animals, Animals, 144
    Grouchy Ladybug, The, 140-142
    Pancakes, Pancakes!, 111-112
    Secret Birthday Message, The, 44
    Very Busy Spider, The, 117-118
    Very Hungry Caterpillar, The, 115, 117
    Very Lonely Firefly, The, 142
Carl's Masquerade, (Day), 87
Catalanotto, P., *Matthew A.B.C.*, 56
"Cat and the Fiddle, The," 40-41
Cherry, L., *Great Kapok Tree, The*, 158
Cinder Edna, (Jackson), 151
Click, Clack, Moo: Cows that Type, (Cronin), 168
comprehension, 6-7
    defined, 137
    lesson overview, 138-139
    research on, 137-138

comprehension lessons
    bookmark technique, 161-164
    discussion web, 170-174
    draw and label retelling, 165-169
    draw and label visualizations, 155-160
    drawing connections, 151-155
    "I wonder" statements, 146-150
    story impressions, 140-145
connections, making, 138, 151-155
Cowley, J., *Mrs. Wishy-Washy's Farm*, 66
Cronin, D.
    Click, Clack, Moo: Cows That Type, 168
    Duck For President, 165-166
    Giggle, Giggle, Quack, 168
Cunningham, P., 66, 79, 182

D

Day, A., *Carl's Masquerade*, 87
Discussion Web, 170-174
Does a Kangaroo Have a Mother Too?, (Carle), 47, 90
Denner, D., 190
Down by the Cool of the Pool, (Mitton), 77
Dr. Seuss's ABC, (Seuss), 22
Duck, Duck, Goose! (A Coyote's on the Loose!), (Beaumont), 36
Duck for President, (Cronin), 165-166
Duke, N., 137

E

Each Peach Pear Plum, (Ahlberg & Ahlberg), 31-32
Eating the Alphabet: Fruits and Vegetables, (Ehlert), 60
Ehlert, L., *Eating the Alphabet: Fruits and Vegetables*, 60
Ehri, L. C., 15-16, 18, 23, 28, 35, 40, 44
evaluating, 139, 170-174
Eric Carle's Animals, Animals, (Carle), 144

F

Farstrup, A., 175
First to Fly, (Busby), 161
Fisher, P., 107, 135
Fleming, D., *Barnyard Banter*, 42
fluency, 6, 80
    defined, 81
    lesson overview, 82-83
    research on, 81-82
fluency lessons
    choral reading, 91-93
    echo reading, 88-90
    fluent reading model, the, 83-87
    Readers Theater, 97-104
    repeated reading, 94-97
Fountas, I., 12, 137
Fowler, A., *Save the Rain Forests*, 127
Fredericks, A., 25, 36
Freedman, C., *Where's Your Smile Crocodile?*, 95
Froggy Goes to School, (London), 68
Frost, H., *Rain Forest Animals Series*, 128
Fyleman, R., "Mice," 83-84

G

Gambrell, L., 12
Gibbons, B., *Nature's Green Umbrella*, 125-126, 128
Gibbons, G.,
    Nature's Green Umbrella, 125-126, 128
    Whales, 130
Giggle, Giggle, Quack, (Cronin), 168
Goudvis, A., 191
graphemes, 6
graphophonic cueing system, 51
Graves, M., 106
Great Kapok Tree, The, (Cherry), 158
Greene, R.G., *This Is the Teacher*, 36
Griffiths, R., *Sharing a Pizza*, 94
Grouchy Ladybug, The, (Carle), 140-142
Growing Up in Coal Country, (Bartoletti), 173
Guided Comprehension Model for the Primary Grades, 7-12
    stages of, 8-9
Guthrie, J., 12

H

Harris, J., *Three Little Dinosaurs, The*, 152-153
Harris, T. L., 15, 51, 81, 107, 137
Harvey, S., 191
Herzog, B., *H is for Home Run*, 170
Hilden, K., 12, 136
H is for Home Run, (Herzog), 170
Hodges, R. E., 15, 51, 81, 107, 137

I

If You Give a Pig a Pancake, (Numeroff), 85
If You Take a Mouse to School, (Numeroff), 83-84
If You Take a Mouse to The Movies, (Numeroff), 86
International Reading Association, 15, 135,176

J

"Jack and Jill," 121-123
Jack and the Meanstalk (Wildsmith), 154
Jackson, E., *Cinder Edna*, 151
James, M., *At the Farmer's Market*, 94
Johnson, D., 195, 196

K

Kamil, M. et al., 175
K Is for Kissing a Cool Kangaroo, (Andreae), 36

L

Literacy Dictionary, The, (Harris & Hodges, eds.), 15
Little Red Hen Makes a Pizza, The, (Sturges), 109-110
London, J., *Froggy Goes to School*, 68
"London Bridge is Falling Down," 20
Low, A., *Aunt Lucy Went to Buy a Hat*, 74
Lucero, J. (That Cat!), 74-75

M

McGinley, W., 190
McLaughlin, M., 7-12, 17, 136, 175, 183, 192, 193, 197, 198, 199
Making Pancakes, (Pritchett), 94
Mama Played Baseball, (Adler), 170, 171
Martin, B.
 Brown Bear, Brown Bear, What Do You See?, 23-24
 Panda Bear, Panda Bear, What Do You See?, 23, 27
 Polar Bear, Polar Bear, What Do You Hear?, 35
Martin's Big Words, (Rappaport), 172
"Mary Had a Little Lamb," 123-124
Matthew A.B.C., (Catalanotto), 56
"Mice," by Fyleman, 83-84
Mitton, T., *Down by the Cool of the Pool*, 77
monitoring, 139, 161-164
Morrow, L., 200
Mrs. Wishy-Washy's Farm, (Cowley), 66-67
My Brothers' Flying Machine, (Yolen), 162

N

Nathan, R., 82
National Commission on Teaching and America's Future, 176
National Reading Panel, 15, 16, 51, 107
Nature's Green Umbrella, (Gibbons), 125-126, 128
Numeroff, L.
 If You Give a Pig a Pancake, 85
 If You Take a Mouse to School, 83-84
 If You Take a Mouse to the Movies, 86
Nunes, S.R., 15-16, 18, 23, 28, 35, 40, 44

O

Oakley, G., 81
Oh, Ducky!, (Slonim), 167
"Old MacDonald Had a Farm," 18-19
Old MacDonald Had a Woodshop, (Shulman), 18-19

P

Padak, N., 81
Palatini, M., *Web Files, The*, 167
Pancakes, Pancakes!, (Carle), 111-112
Panda Bear, Panda Bear, What Do You See?, (Martin), 23
Pearson, P. D., 136, 137, 195, 196
phonemes, 6, 14
phonemic awareness
 defined, 15
 lesson overview, 17
 research, 15-16
phonemic awareness lessons
 phoneme blending, 35-39
 phoneme categorization, 28-34
 phoneme deletion and addition, 44-48
 phoneme identity, 23-28
 phoneme isolation, 18-23
 phoneme segmentation, 40-44
phonics, 50
 defined, 51
 lesson overview, 52
 research, 51

phonics lessons
 alphabet letters and sounds, 53-59
 guess the covered word, 66-69
 making and writing words, 63-66
 making words, 60-63
 onset/rime word wall, 70-73
 word families, 74-78
Pizza the Size of the Sun, A, (Prelutsky), 88
Polar Bear, Polar Bear, What Do You Hear, (Martin), 35
Prelutsky, J.
 Pizza the Size of the Sun, A, 88
 Read-Aloud Rhymes for the Very Young, 83, 95, 96, 179
 Ride a Purple Pelican, 91-92
 Tyrannosaurus Was a Beast, 92
Pressley, M., 12, 136, 137
previewing, 138, 140-145
Pritchett, J., *Making Pancakes*, 94

R

Rain Forest Animals Series, (Frost), 128
Raphael, T., 194
Rappaport, D., *Martin's Big Words*, 172
Rasinski, T. V., 63, 81,105, 182, 183
Read-Aloud Rhymes for the Very Young, (Prelutsky), 83, 95, 96
Richards, M., 105
Ride a Purple Pelican, (Prelutsky), 91-92
"Row, Row, Row Your Boat," 36
Ruddel, R., 176

S

Samuels, S. J., 81, 175, 188
Save the Rain Forests, (Fowler), 127
Schwartz, R., 194
Scieszka, J.
 Squids Will be Squids, 89
 Stinky Cheese Man and Other Fairly Stupid Tales, The, 88
 True Story of the 3 Little Pigs, The, 173
Secret Birthday Message, The, (Carle), 44
self-questioning, 138, 146-150
semantic cueing system, 51
Seuss, Dr., *Dr. Seuss's ABC*, 22
Sharing a Pizza, (Griffiths), 94
Shaw, N., *Sheep in a Jeep*, 47, 76, 179
Sheep in a Jeep, (Shaw), 47, 76, 179
Shulman, L., *Old MacDonald Had a Woodshop*, 18-19
Sierra, J., *Wild About Books*, 36, 39
Simon, S., *Wolves*, 132-133
Slonim, D., *Oh, Ducky*, 167
Snow, C. et al., 15
Squids Will be Squids, (Scieszka), 89
Stahl, S. et al., 79
Stanovich, K., 82
Stinky Cheese Man and Other Fairly Stupid Tales, The, (Scieszka), 88
strategies
 evaluating, 170-174
 making connections, 151-155
 monitoring, 161-164
 previewing, 140-145
 self-questioning, 146-150
 summarizing, 165-169
 visualizing, 155-160
Sturges, P., *Little Red Hen Makes a Pizza, The*, 109-110

Suess, Dr., *Dr. Seuss's ABC*, 22
summarizing, 139, 165-169
syntactic cueing system, 51

T

"That Cat!" by Lucero, 74-75
This Is the Teacher, (Greene), 36, 39
Three Little Dinosaurs, The, (Harris), 152-153
Tompkins, 202
True Story of the 3 Little Pigs, The, (Scieszka), 173
Tyrannosaurus Was a Beast, (Prelutsky), 92

V

Very Busy Spider, The, (Carle), 117-118
Very Hungry Caterpillar, The, (Carle), 115, 117
Very Lonely Firefly, The, (Carle), 142
visualizing, 138, 155-160
vocabulary, 6, 106
 defined, 107
 lesson overview, 108
 research on, 107-108
vocabulary lessons
 concept of definition maps, 115-120
 semantic maps, 109-114
 semantic question map, 125-129
 synonym rhymes, 121-125
 vocabulary bookmark technique, 130-134

W

Watts-Taffe, 106
Web Files, The, (Palatini), 167
Welcome to the Green House, (Yolen), 155
We're Going on a Lion Hunt, (Axtell), 28-30
Whales, (Gibbons), 130
What's the Time, Grandma Wolf?, (Brown), 101-103
"Wheels on the Bus, The," 35
Where's Your Smile Crocodile?, (Freedman), 95
Wigfield, A., 12
Wild About Books, (Sierra), 36, 39
Wildsmith, B., *Jack and the Meanstalk*, 152
Wilson, K., *Bear Wants More*, 70-72
Wolf!, (Bloom), 97-101
Wolves, (Simon), 132-133
words, knowing how words work, 138

Y

Yolen, J.
 My Brothers' Flying Machine, 162
 Welcome to the Green House, 155
Yopp, H. K., 179, 180
Yopp, H. K. & Yopp, R. H., 15-16, 49, 179, 181